DISPROVING CHRISTIANITY

AND OTHER SECULAR WRITINGS

DAVID G. MCAFEE

HYPATIA PRESS

© Copyright David G. McAfee 2019

First Published in the USA 2010 by David G. McAfee as *Disproving Christianity: Refuting the World's Most Followed Religion*

Second edition published in Great Britain 2011 by Dangerous Little Books

Published in the United States of America by Hypatia Press in 2019

ISBN: 978-1-83919-010-0

Cover by Claire Wood

What This Means to Me

Disproving Christianity is important to me, and not *just* because it was my first book. It also means a lot to me because it was my entrance into the world of atheism and secular activism.

I had always been an atheist, but I wasn't really aware of the skeptical communities. I was going to school at UC Santa Barbara and majoring in Religious Studies, and I was still planning on having an academic career in that field. I had never considered becoming an "atheist author" because I didn't know such a thing even existed.

Disproving Christianity didn't start out as a book at all. It began as an essay for personal use. I was taking a class on New Testament literature, combining my loves of writing and learning about religion, and I started to take note of the various contradictions and discrepancies between the books of the Bible. I thought if I wrote an essay with demonstrable errors in the Bible, I could convince my grandparents to give up their positions as Biblical literalists.

I kept writing my personal essay for months, but it continued to evolve beyond what I ever anticipated. Eventually I had about 20 pages of writing, and I started thinking about *other* Biblical literalists I could help if I continued. I kept researching and writing and, at the age of 19, I self-published my book through Amazon. It was called, *Disproving Christianity: Refuting the World' Most Followed Religion*.

I immediately booked a few local speaking events, where I sold some copies of the self-published book, but that was about the extent of my promotional work. Regardless, the book picked up a little bit of steam and I ultimately republished it as *Disproving Christianity and Other Secular Writings* with an imprint know as Dangerous Little Books.

Under the DLB label, *Disproving Christianity* succeeded more than I ever imagined. Perhaps because of the new publisher, or maybe because I gave away more than 40,000 digital copies, positive reviews flooded in. People loved its simplistic style, and the fact that it basically served as a pocket guide for refuting fundamentalist Biblical principles.

It's for that reason that, when the DLB contract expired, I opted to republish with Hypatia Press. I didn't change the content itself—I wanted it to be true to the version people enjoyed—but I thought it deserved a renewed deal and a wider audience. So, feel free to tell all your friends!

Yours in Reason,
David G. McAfee

CONTENTS

PREFACE

The pages that follow will be focused on the fallacies, improbabilities, and contradictions created by the *Christian* tradition—not the idea of a "God" as a whole. Because no one can be *completely certain* that there is no higher power or some other, more abstract, "Creator", it is nearly impossible to 'disprove'; however, it is entirely possible through analysis and research to find discrepancies within the ancient, organized, religious traditions that support the idea of a *specific* god. Each argument and contradiction presented will bring us closer to disproving the main pillars of Christianity using nothing more than logical thinking, statistics, scientific and historical data, and Holy Scriptures. The debates between Christians and non-Christians have raged for thousands of years, and I expect the conflict to continue; but I do hope that these arguments will allow those Christians who may not have questioned biblical fallibility in the past to realize that these texts are man-made, and they represent the ideas of those fallible individuals who created and edited the compilation of texts now considered to be *The Holy Bible*. They contain errors, contradictions, and a stagnant moral code which, in many ways, no longer coincides with the morality of modern man. What I hope to gain from presenting these arguments and little-known biblical passages to the reader is a sense of understanding of scripture which may not be presented in Bible Study or in church—and for good reason. If read with an open mind, I truly believe that this book will open peoples' eyes to the wonders of free thought in a way that other works utilizing a more philosophical approach, cannot. We begin with Christianity primarily because it is the world's most popular religion;[1] adherents of Christian sects compose nearly one-third of the world's population. Although the arguments will not be centered on the dismissal of a God, ideas and theories contradicting a superior Creator (as defined within Christian texts) will also be presented, as they are primary tenets of the Christian religion. Under normal circumstances, disproval of a theory or statement is a relatively simple task; if you find one fault or weakness in the argument upon which the theory rests, it is no longer a valid argument. In this case, however, we will be drawing attention to numerous weaknesses and contradictions—primarily because of the strength that a *religion* can have in one's own mind. The Christian tradition, developed thousands of years ago, has been refined and altered by kings and clergymen alike to fit more appropriately in their time period and culture. With new-age and modern biblical interpretations and translations, this continues even today—it is therefore understandable that, in order to create an appropriate response, *all* weaknesses of *The Bible* must be carefully noted, including scriptural evidence from the New *and* Old Testaments, as well as teachings of modern Christianity.

With so many books of *The Bible* and *numerous* known and unknown authors, *The Holy Bible*'s words create a battlefield within themselves in which contradictory statements are made,

---

[1] According to most authorities, including researcher David B. Barrett's *World Christian Encyclopedia*, the number of Christian adherents (self-identified) is somewhere in between 2.1 billion and 2.2 billion.

translations are forced, and major and minor edits of each account are made to suit the needs of one generation or the next. It is relatively impossible to consider that it would be *flawless* in any edition—but that does not stop some fundamentalist Christians from claiming biblical infallibility. In addition to this critique on biblical literalism, I will also show evidence that the very *concepts* of Christianity, acts of God, pillars of belief, and contemporary teachings are contradictory in themselves, in addition to the unnecessary violence, absurd statements, and ideas that we find ridiculous today that are so common in New Testament and Hebrew scriptures. Each of these ideas will be brought to light using biblical evidence; though *every* argument and contradiction will not make it into this book, there will be enough to inform the average person who is unaware of the true teachings of the "sacred" Bible. The evidence for doctrinal contradictions will include passages from *The Bible* as a whole (as opposed to solely analyzing the New Testament) because the Hebrew scriptures (what Christians refer to as the "Old Testament") are no less important and influential to modern Christianity than the New Testament containing the acts of Jesus Christ, as his own words indicate in Matthew 5:17: "Think not that I come to destroy the law, or the prophets: I am not come to destroy, but to fulfill." The canonical books of the Torah and other Hebrew scriptures compose the first (and the majority) part of the Christian Bible today—in all versions—ensuring that its laws and commandments are taken as divine law to all Christian followers.

Before disproving (or even debating) a theory or idea—in this case, we will be discussing a religious tradition—one must first accomplish a few tasks. The first of these is to define that which is to be disproven or discussed; as Socrates once said, "The beginning of wisdom is a definition of terms."[2] Following this principle, definitions will continue to be a crucial component of this text because accepted meanings are the keys to universal understanding, without which nothing can be proven or disproven. In this particular instance it is necessary to settle on a universal definition of "Christianity" in order to create and pursue a successful argument. For this I have developed a simple yet concise definition: Christianity, for the purposes of this book, will be considered *the organized belief system based on the life and teachings of Jesus of Nazareth and utilizing the Old and New Testaments of The Bible as the literal word of God.* This definition is carefully crafted to include the following *sects* of Christianity: Catholic, Protestant, Eastern Orthodox, Pentecostal, Anglican, Latter-day Saints, Evangelical, Quakers, and *many* more. Though some more liberal Christians do not consider *The Bible* as a literal work, but a metaphorical one, the sacredness of the tradition relies on these compiled texts—without which the entire religion would cease to exist, as it is the only recorded account of the events which supposedly occurred. Therefore it remains important to outline the outdated ideas that the book teaches and show why—even as a metaphorical scripture—*The Bible* teaches ideas which are increasingly irrelevant and even counter-productive as our social morality and scientific understanding of the world evolves on a global scale. As *The Bible* is the central piece of literature upon which all Christian morals and ideas are based, it is also necessary to use one

---

[2] Quote attributed to Socrates (Σωκράτης), a classical Greek philosopher (c. 469 BC-399 BC).

common type or translation. Though it is not the earliest English translation, nor is it by any means the most recent, the Authorized King James Version of *The Bible*, created in 1611, is the most widely accepted among Christian traditions[3]; therefore it will be cited in the chapters that follow as the *Word of God*. There will be various citations and references for Bible verses on many of the arguments; feel free to follow along.

Once all definitions have been established, only then is it safe to present evidence; as far as Christianity is concerned, through *The Bible* and religious discourse, the evidence for "proof" of these supernatural claims—or the Christian *thesis*—has already been submitted. These claims, as I intend to show, fail to meet the burden of *proof*, which is why faith is considered an acceptable substitute for logic and reason in the Christian tradition. However, this reliance on that which cannot be proven will not stop us from examining the claims of the Christian Bible, as well as the teachings of Christian churches of various denominations, in a logical manner in order to create a successful counterargument. Keep in mind that it is much easier to *falsify* a claim than it is to *verify* one beyond a reasonable doubt; this makes our task a relatively simple one. A successful argument will show that the Christian religion, as it is understood today and expressed through *The Holy Bible*, is *not* the literal word of God and contains a plethora of contradictions that would make such a claim *impossible*.

Though many believers in the Christian faith will either disregard the evidence put forth in this book *or* attempt to refute it, it is

---

[3] Though the New International Version of *The Bible* is becoming increasingly more popular, the lack of copyright protections and traditional significance of the King James Version contribute to its success within the Christian canon.

impossible to effectively argue the validity of an ancient document that has so many weaknesses and problems. Now, using this biblical critique, we are able to document *many* of the fallacies and atrocities canonized within the scripture itself, and taught by missionaries and clergymen across the world. Each argument that follows carefully notates references within *The Holy Bible*—citing chapter and verse within the text—ensuring that everyone can follow along as we '*disprove Christianity*'.

The Bible is abundantly clear that it is composed of the infallible words of a perfect God, meaning that *any* imperfections can essentially disprove the book and, therefore, the religion. Most Evangelical and Protestant groups subscribe to a belief in biblical inerrancy—in other words, the Word of God (Bible) is infallible and perfect—and *any* inaccuracies are impossible, creating an easily refuted thesis. It is however, as previously mentioned, still necessary to document as many instances as possible of these contradictory statements, absurd claims, and historical misrepresentations in order to completely disprove the doctrine of Christianity as a viable, historically accurate, representation of true events— especially those biblical errors that are not overly popular or otherwise overlooked in mainstream biblical critiques. But before we present the evidence *against* the Holy Scriptures, we must first prove that *The Bible* is *meant* to be taken as the literal word of a flawless Lord. The biblical evidence is very clear in this regard; for example, John 10:35 states (emphasis added), *"If he called them gods, unto whom the word of God came, **and the scripture cannot be broken,** "* and the Second Epistle of Peter 1:21 claims that *The Bible* was not written by men in saying that *"the prophecy came not in old* *time by the will of man: but holy men of God spake as they were moved by the Holy Ghost.* "Last, but certainly not least, *Revelation 22:19* claims that *"if any man shall take away from the words of the book of this prophecy, God shall take away his part out of the book of life, and out of the holy city, and from the things which are written in this book."*

PART ONE

DISPROVING CHRISTIANITY: REFUTING THE WORLD'S MOST FOLLOWED RELIGION

CULTURAL CHRISTIANITY

In America, most people identify with the Christian religion...yet I am not convinced that those "adherents" a) *know* what it means to be a Christian and understand the historical and metaphorical *baggage* that comes with such a label, and b) actually *follow* the biblical teachings associated with the religion. My interest in the field of *cultural Christianity* began two years ago during an interview with a university student for a local magazine. His name was Mike and he was a second-year theater major at the University of California, Santa Barbara. I had the chance to speak candidly with Mike and used that opportunity to put to him a series of questions regarding his religious preferences and freedoms. His answer to one question in particular would surprise me more than the rest. I asked Mike a very simple question: "Do you consider yourself a religious person?" A 2001 American Religious Identification Survey indicates that 81% of Americans *do* associate themselves with a specific religion—76% self-identify with Christianity[4]—so a "Yes" would not have been cause for alarm. Instead, Mike paused for a moment and answered, "I'm half Christian and half agnostic." Before I responded, my mind was filled with ideas of what he *could* have meant; some blend of Catholic intrigue mixed with skepticism perhaps? Upon elaboration I discovered

—

[4] 86% of Americans self-identified as Christians in 1990 and 76 % in 2008: http://www.americanreligionsurvey-aris.org.

that Mike's mother was a practicing Protestant and his father was not associated with an organized religion—alarmingly, he indicated that this made him "half Christian and half agnostic."

When I describe this concept of one's religious identity, I often refer to it as the "genetics" of religion; I am referring to a phenomenon that I came across during the course of my research in Religious Studies that, to me, demonstrates that religion can be something similar to genetic inheritance in the rates at which is passed on from generation to generation via the parents. For example, people who have extremely limited knowledge of *The Bible* or its implications may still choose to classify themselves as "Christians" on the basis that their parents do so—they may never even give it a second thought. This phenomenon of our nation's children inheriting religion is often overlooked because the perpetrator guilty of indoctrination is not a dictator or cult leader, but instead it is most often their own parents or close family members. In the course of my research *and* daily life, it became increasingly apparent that many Americans consider themselves "Christians" with *extremely* limited knowledge of the beliefs and practices of the particular religion simply because of their parents, peers, and/or popular culture.

When a child is growing up, there is a crucial period in which he or she begins to ask questions about life and wonder about the origin of existence. This also happens to be a time in which the curious child learns about his or her surroundings and is most impressionable. In a religious family, these questions are typically answered in a *religious* context—whether the ideas are introduced in the home, church, or Sunday school. Once these beliefs are instilled in the child, it often becomes a part of his or her identity; so much so that, in many cases, the child will grow up and forever identify him or herself with that specific religion without question or skepticism—after all, these ideas were introduced by a loving and trusted family member, leaving little incentive to doubt their validity. This is not to say that *all* religious parents pass on their faith to their offspring, but it seems as if it is just as likely as inheriting hair or eye color. For an idea as important as religion, it is a shame that Americans (and people around the world) simply take what they are taught from family at face value as opposed to studying, questioning, and learning about multiple religious traditions in order to make an informed decision regarding how, if at all, these organized belief systems will play a role in their own lives. I often ask Christians who received their religious ideologies from family whether or not they acknowledge the statistical assumption that if they had been born in, say, India—to Indian parents—for example, they would probably be affiliated with a denomination of Hinduism instead of the Christian tradition which they now consider to be the absolute Truth, though they would likely hold these religious beliefs with equal or rivaled fervor.

It seems to me that more and more people are treating their religious affiliation as if it *were* an inherited trait, as opposed to an individual right and a decision not to be taken lightly. The momentous event of choosing a religion, or lack of religion, should not be a mindless reflex but a carefully scrutinized moment in life... and the key to this moment, as it is in many crucial decisions, is information. When a child is raised in religion, it eliminates the *choice* in what is arguably the most important decision one can make in a lifetime—the decision of which religion, if any, to follow. While researching this topic, I spoke to a Catholic priest regarding the issue of cultural Christianity; he wished to be referred to only as "John." John responded by making the point that religion is the only way to teach our young children "how to be moral" in today's society; I personally believe that we are better than this. Morals *do* exist outside of organized religion, and the "morality" taught by many of these archaic systems is often outdated, sexist, racist, and teaches intolerance and inequality.[5] When a parent forces a child into a religion, the parent is effectively handicapping his or her own offspring by limiting the abilities of the child to question the world around him or her and make informed decisions. Children raised under these conditions will mature believing that *their* religion is the only correct one, and, in the case of Christianity, they will believe that all who doubt their religion's validity will suffer eternal damnation. This environment is one that often breeds hate, ignorance, and "justified" violence. This concept of cultural Christianity closes the minds of *some* believers—making our task of disproving Christianity to the lay believer a difficult, yet necessary, endeavor.

—

5 For more information, see chapter eight entitled: "Atrocities and Absurdities Committed or Condoned by the Lord."

A Brief Introduction to Christianity in America

As stated in the preface, Christianity is the world's most popular religion and therefore a logical choice for beginning a method of disproval for other supernatural claims. In the United States of America, the Christian tradition is so overwhelmingly prevalent that it has influenced our laws, our nation's formation, political appointments, and many other aspects of daily life. The United States of America is the land of freedom; our federal Constitution even guarantees the citizens of this nation the freedom of religion, speech, the press, and individual opportunity to pursue happiness. The Constitution also guarantees the freedom to be governed by a secular political system, commonly known as the *separation of church and state*;[6] this simply means that our government should be free of religious influences in order to avoid a nation oppressed by a religious majority much like the one that our Constitution's framers had escaped. One may see that, on the surface, the American government is primarily a secular entity in that America, unlike some countries, does not have a national religion, but many

---

[6] Thomas Jefferson, in a letter to a group of Danbury Baptists: "I contemplate with sovereign reverence that act of the whole American people which declared that their legislature should make no law respecting an establishment of religion, or prohibiting the free exercise thereof, thus building a wall of separation between church and state."

things about this country's formation, monetary systems, and laws are anything but secular and are undeniably influenced by Christianity.

THE PRINCIPLE AMERICA WAS BUILT UPON

The attitude of many early Christian missionaries who helped shape today's society was that of Christian superiority. Many of these early settlers sought to destroy any Native American who refused to convert to Christianity or came in between them and their God-given destiny. "Manifest destiny" is the belief that many Americans shared in the early 1800s that it was America's "destiny" to control the entire North American continent. To many early American settlers, this meant that it was God's will that the United States of America expand its territory from the East Coast to the West Coast. These early Christian *Puritans* thought that by colonizing the West Coast, they would bring their Christian values and ideals to the "uncivilized" native residents. In actuality, what they brought instead was death, disease, and many other hardships focused mainly on the Native American "savages" that inhabited much of this area during that time. Manifest destiny was far too often used as a tool of justification for cruelty and unethical treatment of the 'godless' Native Americans. These natives were thought of as inferior beings because of their lack of organized religion and primitive lifestyles. This foundation of Christian superiority in America has continued throughout history and, to this day, every president of the United States has been a Christian[7] (though some clearly more devout than others) and, in some cases, thanked Jesus for being specifically responsible for America's greatness, often at the sacrifice of other nations. Forty-third President and Methodist Christian George W. Bush stated his belief that God is watching over America by saying, *"Our Founders thanked the Almighty and humbly sought His wisdom and blessing. May we always live by that same trust, and may God continue to watch over and bless the United States of America."*[8] This "God is on our side" mentality has carried over into our political and military actions as well: it is often said that God is watching over our soldiers and it is God's will to spread our brand of democracy. When I hear these words from our elected leaders, I cringe in disbelief at how history does, indeed, repeat itself. I think of the tribal Native Americans forced to forget their own traditions and adopt Christianity or die; I think of every war and taken life justified using God's name.

AMERICAN MONEY

Although the idea of an American government with a Christian agenda began in the early times of our settlers, it has continued until this very day with the printing and coining of American

---

[7] It is often argued that many early American Presidents had agnostic or non-religious tendencies, including Abraham Lincoln. However, official documentation is clear that these men were— at least at some point— self-identified Christians.

[8] George W. Bush, November 21, 2003. http://georgewbush-whitehouse.archives.gov/news/releases/2003/11/20031121-10.html

currency. "In God We Trust" appears on all forms of American money from the penny to the one-hundred-dollar bill. Similarly to the Christian version of the Pledge of Allegiance, the U.S. government began printing "In God We Trust" on all American legal tender as a way to increase religious sentiment in a time of conflict. This addition to our currency was made during the Civil War as the nation's Christian population increased dramatically. According to the secretary of the Treasury in 1861, he began to receive an influx of letters demanding that the Union make a coin recognizing citizens' faith. The first of these letters was written to Secretary Chase by Rev. M. R. Watkinson, minister of the Gospel, from Pennsylvania. In this letter, Reverend Watkinson states that by producing such a coin, "This would relieve us from the ignominy of heathenism. This would place us openly under the Divine protection we have personally claimed."9 The "In God We Trust" motto first appeared on an American two-cent coin in 1864. In 1837, an act of Congress declared that any motto printed on American currency is the sole decision of Congress. This means that the mint could not make any changes without additional legislation through the legislative branch. The legislative branch of our federal government controls the printing of money and, though it raises much controversy, the presses continue to print the phrase on all American legal tender (on paper currency since 1957). This is a true example of Christianity in the American federal government. Congress has upheld its decision to continue printing the phrase as an "American tradition."

---

9 http://www.treasury.gov/about/education/Pages/in-god-we-trust.aspx

AMERICAN LAWS

Though it may be less clear at times than "one nation under God" or "In God We Trust," many other—similarly controversial—issues continue to arise from the Christianity-based moral fabric that is woven into American society through laws. Because America is a democratic nation, the majority rules; therefore it is not surprising that everything from the laws that we make to our everyday life choices are somehow connected with Christianity; this is not a necessarily good or bad relationship, but a statement of fact. It is because of our Christian majority in America, as well as the increasing power of specific churches and those who lobby politically on behalf of church groups, that we continue to see a lapse in separation of church and state through our federal laws involving abortion, the definition of marriage, and embryonic stem cell research. The outlawing of same-sex marriage in most states is often considered a *religious* matter by those who condemn the union of homosexual couples. Citing biblical scripture and chanting "Adam and Eve—not Adam and Steve" is far too often seen in attempts to further the agenda of many religious activists against the practice of gay marriage. And as much as "modern" and "progressive" Christians attempt to deny it, the fact of the matter is that *The Bible does* condemn homosexuality in various verses and chapters throughout the Old and New Testaments. The most cited example is in Leviticus 18:22: "*Thou shalt not lie with mankind, as with womankind: it is an abomination.*" But there are plenty of verses that indicate that those who participate in such *sinful* acts are to be condemned to hell and will *not* inherit the kingdom of

God, including Leviticus 20:13[10] and 1 Corinthians 6:9-10.[11] The Christian majority is seemingly allowing ancient scripture indicating that homosexuals should be put to death as a tool to circumvent the civil rights of mankind, a practice that occurs far too often within Christianity and any branch of religious fundamentalism.

A woman's right to choose is commonly known as the right for a woman to choose whether or not to terminate a pregnancy while it is in a nonviable state (nonviable is defined as not capable of living, growing, or developing and functioning successfully)[12]. Abortion laws are, at this time, determined at the state level as opposed to the federal level. This means that each state may create its own laws determining who should be able to receive an abortion, at which time an abortion should be legal, and whether spousal or parental consent is required for an abortion, as long as the states abide by the federal Constitution by not allowing abortions during the third trimester. This debate, from a non-religious viewpoint, is *only* a personal matter, but that doesn't stop the religiously-motivated among us to attempt to reframe the questions as a *religious* and *political* matter. Many Christian politicians find the practice of abortion to be "against God" and therefore fight to impose their religious ideologies into this matter

---

[10] Leviticus 20:13: "If a man also lie with mankind, as he lieth with woman, both of them have committed an abomination: they shall surely be put to death; their blood shall be upon them."

[11] 1 Corinthians 6:9-10: "Know ye not that the unrighteous shall not inherit the kingdom of God? Be not deceived: neither fornicators, nor idolaters, nor adulterers, nor effeminate, nor abusers of themselves with mankind, nor thieves, nor covetous, nor drunkards, nor revilers, nor extortioners, shall inherit the kingdom of God."

[12] http://www.nlm.nih.gov/medlineplus/mplusdictionary.html

through legislation. And there are many (usually right-winged) *religious* activists who cite biblical scripture claiming that abortion is equivalent to murder and even advocate on behalf of federal laws and constitutional amendments prohibiting any abortions, including in extenuating circumstances. It should not be surprising, then, that with a Christian majority we would expect to see this type of practice completely outlawed on the basis of religion alone. However, abortion continues to be available for women who seek it during the first trimester and, with some exceptions, into the second trimester. During the second trimester of pregnancy, because the risk to the mother's health grows larger for an abortion during this time, the state *"may regulate the abortion procedure in ways that are reasonably related to maternal health."* During the third trimester, because the Supreme Court has determined that a fetus becomes viable at this time, the state may choose to regulate or even prohibit abortions. These laws, as established by the Supreme Court, are under attack every day by fundamentalist religionists who claim that the parents and physicians are "playing God." Some high-profile Christian politicians have even cited their Christian faith as a reason for not supporting abortions for victims of rape or in instances in which the mother's life is at risk.

Traditional Christian values are thought to promote peace, love, "turning the other cheek,"[13] and following the life of the Christ. This is all too often forgotten when Christian *extremists* and fanatics take their personal beliefs too far; this is when they choose to forget about "turning the other cheek" and embrace

---

[13] Matthew 5:39: "But I say unto you, That ye resist not evil: but whosoever shall smite thee on thy right cheek, turn to him the other also."

more dangerous scripture—perhaps they take the contradictory, yet equally 'Christian', approach of "*Eye for eye, tooth for tooth, hand for hand, foot for foot.*"[14] This is extremely obvious in the fight against a woman's right to choose by extremist religionists who take dangerous and radical stands against the practice of abortion. Women have been killed, abortion clinics have been bombed, doctors have been attacked, and in some cases women have been denied medical care because they terminated a pregnancy. This act of Christian terrorism is the same terrorism that we have been fighting *against* in the Middle East, but it is taking shape as a result of interpretation of Christian scriptures, not Muslim texts. America is blindly in denial to these acts of terrorism and violence in our own country and refuse to acknowledge these Christian terrorist extremists as such. The separation of church and state continues to be a phantom in American society today; however, I believe that one day our nation will realize its potential by living up to its Constitution and becoming a truly free country without unfairly distributed theistic influences in legislature.

This chapter does not even begin to analyze the depth to which Christian values penetrate our nation's laws and political structure, but it does provide an introductory look at the theocratic influence that the United States of America has overcome and then emulated, and shows the importance of the disproval of such a destructive tradition for the safety and well-being of America and the global community. We will begin the debunking of Christianity with a *philosophical* flaw found in any religion that ensures the

———

14 Exodus 21:24: "Eye for eye, tooth for tooth, hand for hand, foot for foot,"

spread of the belief system by embedding acceptance requirements into the doctrine. For example, if you are a Christian and believe the words of *The Holy Bible*, you believe that everyone who does not believe as you do will suffer eternal damnation. This is an archaic concept that many traditions utilize in order to *scare* people into believing. In this fashion, *The Bible and* its adherents are using fear to convert people to Christianity. My name for this particular idea is the "morality versus worship" argument.

MORALITY VERSUS WORSHIP

"Live a good life. If there are gods and they are just, then they will not care how devout you have been, but will welcome you based on the virtues you have lived by. If there are gods, but unjust, then you should not want to worship them. If there are no gods, then you will be gone, but will have lived a noble life that will live on in the memories of your loved ones."[15]

I would like to begin with this quotation because it outlines very eloquently one of the most popular arguments against Christianity, though it can be applied to many theistic traditions. Christians often preach, and The Bible states, that there are prerequisites for entrance into heaven beyond simply following the moral teachings of The Bible as you might interpret it, including the requirement of having accepted Jesus of Nazareth as Lord and Savior.[16] The Bible explicitly indicates that acceptance of Jesus as Lord is a necessary condition for entry to heaven in John 14:6: "I am the way, and the truth, and the life; no one comes to the Father but through Me." This verse is, however, only one of the many indicating the necessity not of moral behavior to be saved, but of accepting Jesus Christ—who, according to doctrine, is supposed to have lived thousands of years ago and for whose

---

[15] Quote by Marcus Aurelius, Roman emperor (26 April 121- 17 March 180).
[16] John 14:6: "For God so loved the world, that he gave his only begotten Son, that whosoever believeth in him should not perish, but have everlasting life."

existence we have little-to-no evidence, neither as a man nor as part of the divine Christian God-head. It is on the basis of this acceptance requirement that missionaries began their crusades to spread the word of Christ, because those who have not heard the true word of Jesus would be sure to suffer eternal damnation. From this we can infer two things: firstly, that those who have heard of Jesus the Christ and deny him will not receive the gift of eternal communion with God; and, secondly, that those who have not heard of the teachings of Jesus will likewise be condemned as all humans are sinners according to this tradition and, in order to be forgiven for any sins, you must accept that Jesus Christ is God incarnate.

According to missionary authorities,[17] somewhere around 2.74 billion people have not heard the "gospel of Christ" and are therefore subject to the punishment of God. The problem with this lack of Christian universalism lies within the worship/morality barrier. Would a just God sentence a morally good individual to hell for never having heard of him? And for that matter, would a just God expel a morally good individual to hell who has heard of Jesus, but simply finds no evidentiary reason to believe? According to any reasonable interpretation of Christianity's key doctrines, the answer is a simple and firm "yes". This is because, according to Christian dogma, it is impossible to be "moral" without Jesus Christ; I disagree with this on a fundamental level. It seems to me that this claim indicates that if a Christian were to lose his or her faith, he or she would no longer know right from wrong—a scary concept, to say the least. Yet, if there exists a person who follows

---

[17] Statistics according to "The Joshua Project" global mission statistics.

biblical moral code strictly but doesn't believe in Jesus' divinity, the "merciful"[18] Christian God promises eternal damnation. If it is the case that nonbelievers are punished based solely on nonbelief, and this is the purpose for early Christian missionaries to spread the Gospel, then we can conclude that those individuals who haven't heard or cannot understand the teachings will be likewise damned. The problem is therefore extended from nonbelievers to those ignorant of Christ's teachings to those incapable of believing due to mental defect or age. For example, because The Bible teaches that no man is without sin[19] and does not mention the specific status of children in the afterlife, it is easy to conclude that, logically, children who die when they are too young to know of Christ's word may not have a place in eternal communion with God. This debate led to various sects creating new Christian teachings promoting different purgatories and limbo-like layers of afterlife for unbaptized children. Many "modern" Christians stray away from this rather unpopular concept, but the fact remains that, biblically, it is impossible to enter heaven without first accepting Jesus Christ as Lord and Savior. The requirement to obey and acknowledge God and Jesus Christ has caused the teachings of the Christian tradition to stray from morality to idol worship, creating a world in which a murderer can be forgiven and sent to heaven, whereas a loving and caring skeptic would be cast into damnation.

Not only do I believe that it is possible to maintain moral standards without the crutch of religion—but I would argue that it

---

[18] Luke 6:36: "Be ye therefore merciful, as your Father also is merciful."
[19] 1 Kings 8:46: "For there is no man that sinneth not."

is the only way to achieve true goodness and express real altruism. Free from the constraints of organized religion, a human being is able to express decency from one's self—as opposed to attempting to appease whatever higher power he or she may believe in. By separating worship and morality, we can act in accordance with our own human morals and be able to be less selfish in our motivations for kindness and moral behaviors.

MAINSTREAM THEORIES OF DISPROVAL

Here I will present some of the most famous arguments (accompanied by some new theories of my own) *against* the principles of Christianity, including the concepts of monotheism, heaven and hell, free will, destiny, and more. From philosophical ideas to scientific evidence, these arguments compose the primary examples of weaknesses in logical thinking behind the teachings of the world's most followed tradition.

A. The *Natural Disaster* Argument—Again, I'd like to begin by introducing a relevant quote: *"Is God willing to prevent evil, but not able? Then he is not omnipotent. Is he able, but not willing? Then he is malevolent. Is he both able and willing? Then whence cometh evil? Is he neither able nor willing? Then why call him God?"*[20] Many scholars and philosophers have attempted to disprove the existence of an omniscient, omnipresent, and omnipotent God (as described in the Christian tradition)[21] by simply asking why such a God would allow bad things to happen to his creations. This argument is often dubbed "The Problem of Evil" and is easily combated with the statement that humans cause evil as acts of free will. However, *natural* disasters (also called "acts of God") have no place in this counterpoint. If a just, merciful, omnipotent God existed and loved all mankind, it is difficult to fathom why such a loving

---

[20] Epicurus, Greek philosopher, BC 341-270.
[21] Revelation 19:6: "Alleluia: For the Lord God omnipotent reigneth."

Creator would not only *allow* these disasters to occur and kill innocent nonbelievers and believers alike, but actually *cause* them.[22] This is not considered a radical interpretation of scripture as some of the most well-known Christian Evangelists believe that this is the case, even blaming Hurricane Katrina and other natural disasters on the sinful behavior of those affected by the catastrophes. Graphically, this argument is displayed as such:

1. We have established that the religion of Christianity presupposes an omnipotent, omniscient, omnipresent, omnibenevolent God and Creator.

2. *If* a Creator *knew all, saw all, controlled all,* and *loved all,* said Creator would not allow innocent men, women, and children (especially those who are too young to have sinned) to die by natural disasters or disease.

3. Because we know that innocent men, women, and infants, Christians and non-Christians alike, *do* indeed die by acts of God on a daily basis, we know that an all-loving and all-powerful God must *not* exist.

4. Therefore, Christianity, which proposes the idea of such a Creator, must not be an accurate representation of true events.

———

[22] Nahum 1:3-6: "The LORD is slow to anger, and great in power, and will not at all acquit the wicked: the LORD hath his way in the whirlwind and in the storm, and the clouds are dust of his feet. He rebuketh the sea, and maketh it dry, and drieth up all the rivers: Bashan languisheth, and Carmel, and the flower of Lebanon languisheth. The mountains quake at him, and the hills melt, and the earth is burned at his presence, yea, the world, and all that dwell therein. Who can stand before his indignation? And who can abide in the fierceness of his anger? His fury is poured out like fire, and the rocks are thrown down by him."

b. The *Loved Ones* Argument—The Loved Ones Argument is a basic yet concise example of a philosophical disproval method. In order to further explain this idea, we must first define the term *"heaven"*, from a Christian perspective. Heaven, in *The Bible*, is described as a paradise[23] in which one is to live in eternal communion with God; it is considered to be a place of complete bliss incomparable to the experiences on earth. I don't know many Christians that would disagree with this definition or characterization. Once the definition of heaven is established, the question arises for the believer as to the destiny of those closest to the Christian, who may or may not agree with his or her specific religious ideologies. Many people acknowledge that there exists the possibility of a connection between two people so strong that true happiness cannot exist *without* that other person. If two people who cannot experience their ideal "paradise" without one another die, one being a believer and one a skeptic, we can infer that the Christian will go to heaven and the other to hell. Because the believer can *only* be truly happy with this other individual, heaven would become contradictory (no longer paradise) because of the separation. In my own humble opinion, I believe that even "heaven" would be a *personal* hell without my loved ones, especially when you imagine the horror of *knowing* that your loved ones are burning for eternity while you bask in God's glory. Again, I will display the argument visually in order to ensure a more clear understanding by all.

---

[23] 2 Corinthians 12:2-4: "I knew a man in Christ above fourteen years ago...such an one caught up to the third heaven. And I knew such a man... How that he was caught up into paradise, and heard unspeakable words, which it is not lawful for a man to utter."

1. Heaven, as described by the Christian tradition, is eternal happiness in communion with God.

2. It possible that, because of nothing more than a difference in beliefs, two people whose ideal "heaven" included one another could be separated in the afterlife and one could be sent to "heaven" without his or her significant other.

3. The Christian in heaven could *not* be happy without his or her loved one, thus causing heaven to become a place of everlasting pain and sadness.

4. Because heaven is described as eternal *happiness*, this creates a contradiction in which the concept of a Christian heaven fails to be viable.

5. Therefore Christianity, which ensures eternal bliss in heaven postmortem, cannot be the true word of an all-knowing and loving God.

C. The *Jesus on the Cross* Argument—Most sects of modern Christianity preach that God sent his only begotten son to earth in order to be crucified for man's sins. Scriptural evidence of this includes a passage from John 10:17, 18: "*Therefore doth my Father love me, because I lay down my life…No man taketh it from me, but I lay it down myself…This commandment have I received of my Father.*"[24] Because of Jesus' supposed predestination, God would have had to choose the people who would kill and betray his son, choose the method by which he would be killed (crucifixion), and

---

[24]John 10:17, 18: "Therefore doth my Father love me, because I lay down my life, that I might take it again. No man taketh it from me, but I lay it down of myself. I have the power to lay it down, and I have the power to take it again. This commandment have I received of my Father."

the time at which the event would occur. Those guilty of *killing* Jesus would therefore be simply carrying out God's wishes without the free will to have chosen a path for themselves. The problem with this lies in the fate of the Romans who physically killed Jesus Christ and, for that matter, Judas Iscariot who is said to have betrayed him. Simply ask yourself, did these betrayers of Christ go to heaven—or do they now reside in hell? If one is to say that the men guilty of this trespass against the Lord went to *heaven,* Christianity's primary tenet would be contradicted: one must first *accept* Jesus before entrance into heaven. These men clearly did not accept Jesus as a savior. If one is to decide that the men went to *hell,* it causes another problem with the Christian idea of free will. Because God *sent* his son to be crucified, he had to have ensured that someone (the Romans) would do it, removing the free will from these men; and punishing them with eternal damnation for something that God, by definition, planned.

D. The *Origins of the Universe* Argument—One of the most common arguments in *favor* of Christianity and monotheism evokes the nontheists' inability to explain the origin of the universe in accurate and definite terms. Usually it begins with a theist—in this case we will say a Christian—asking a nonbeliever about the origins of the universe with an emphasis on *what happened before the big bang.* This is, clearly, a circular argument because neither party has an explanation for what could have happened before creation or formation, though there are many hypotheses. In order to demonstrate the counterargument that utilizes the believer's same logic, I will reproduce the philosophical debate in the form of a dialogue.

Christian: "Where did the universe come from, if not from a loving Creator?"

Nonbeliever: "Why did it have to come from anything?"

Christian: "Everything has to come from something."

Nonbeliever: "Then, you tell me: where did the universe come from?"

Christian: "The universe came from God."

Nonbeliever: "Where did God come from?"

Christian: "God did not have to come from anything…he always was."

Nonbeliever: "Then everything does not have to come from something. Perhaps the universe always was."

ε. The *Age of the Earth* Contradiction—This issue has been a hotly contested one amongst scientists, historical scholars, and religious authorities for many years. The problem lies within the wording of *The Bible*, which seemingly indicates that the earth has been around fewer than seven thousand years from its creation until today. If *The Bible* is to be considered, as it is taught by the majority of Christian clergymen, as the *literal* word of God, and all of its statements truthful, then this *should* mean that scientific evidence would support such claims; in this instance, that is not the case. Using various radiometric dating methods, scientists have discovered parts of earth's crust to be around 3.8 billion years old, but experts generally agree that the earth is over 4.5 billion years old.[25] Because we *know* that the earth cannot be less than ten thousand years of age, the only question is whether or not *The*

---

[25] U.S. Geological Survey, 1997, http://pubs.usgs.gov/gip/geotime/age.html

Bible explicitly makes that claim. Here I will outline the chapters that indicate that indeed it does.

1. In Genesis, the first book of the Old Testament, a description of the earth's creation by God includes man, woman, fish, beasts, sky, lightness, darkness, earth, and, after God creates humanity, states: "And the evening and the morning were the sixth day."[26] We conclude, then, that *The Bible* literally represents the earth as being five days older than humanity.

2. In Luke 3:23-38, Luke gives a detailed ancestry of Jesus, beginning with his father and outlining seventy-two generations between Adam (and the creation of earth) and Jesus Christ. Historians are able to document the approximate time period between Abraham and Jesus, which the Bible says is fifty-three generations. If the Bible were correct, this would be around two thousand years.

3. Using lifespan averages (most of the chronology is available through Genesis 5:3-27,[27] in which Adam is linked to Noah, including the number of years each father lived), we can calculate that the remaining twenty generations between Abraham and Adam *also* constitutes approximately two thousand years.

---

[26] Genesis 1:31-2:02: "And the evening and the morning were the sixth day. Thus the heavens and the earth were finished, and all the host of them. And on the seventh day God ended his work which he had made; and he rested on the seventh day from all his work which he had made."

[27] Genesis 5:5-11: "And all of the days that Adam lived were nine hundred and thirty years: and he died...And all the days of Seth were nine hundred and twelve years...And all the days of Enos were nine hundred and five years: and he died."

To summarize, the earth itself was created just five days earlier than man. Two thousand years and twenty generations later, Abraham is born and later has a son named Isaac. Fifty-three generations (much shorter than in prior generations in which some of the ancestors are reported to have lived to be over nine-hundred years old[28]) and two-thousand years follow until God gives Mary the gift of conception without having known man's touch, the virgin birth. Using rough estimates, biblical scholars and fundamentalist Christian churches agree that *The Bible* estimates an approximate time of between 6,000 and 7,000 years since the beginning of the earth's creation according to the Old and New Testaments. Because modern science has taught us that this *cannot* be true, we can infer that *The Bible*, and therefore the Christian religion, does not accurately represent the history of events of the earth's origin.

ᖵ. *The Modern Miracle Argument*—some non-Christians argue that the lack of *miracles* in modern society proves that the Judeo-Christian monotheistic God either doesn't exist or has simply become inactive. This argument is simple and met with much skepticism within the religious community; the attempted refutation of *this* statement usually comes in the form of modern healing. For example, if a believer has a family member or friend afflicted with some sort of fatal disease and it is cured or it enters remission, many believers claim that God saved the person's life and cured the disease; therefore God *does* perform miracles every day—they are just on a much smaller scale than is depicted in *The Bible*. If this is

---

[28] Genesis 5:27: "And all the days of Methuselah were nine hundred sixty and nine years: and he died."

true and God enters the lives of *some* individuals in order to heal them, why wouldn't he heal someone with a more obvious problem—like an amputee who is missing an appendage? According to this logic, God is credited for helping some people (possibly millions) who suffer from diseases, but has never healed a single amputee or anyone suffering from a life-threatening but physically visible issue. This leaves us to conclude that either a) God heals *some* people but chooses to help none facing fatal physical disabilities (this contradicts the "all-loving" aspect of the Christian God), or b) that God *cannot* heal a physical disability (this contradicts the presupposed omnipotence of God). In either outcome, we see that the idea for modern miracles cannot be considered an adequate argument for an *active* God.

G. *Disproving the Concept of an Infallible God*—this is a relatively simple concept regarding the ability of God to make mistakes. Scripturally, we can infer that God is *perfect* (see *Matthew 5:48: "Be ye therefore perfect, even as your Father which is in heaven is perfect"*). The idea of an infallible God is universally accepted among the Christian sects, yet it is clear from various biblical passages (and, some would argue, everyday events) that God can regret, repent,[29] feel jealousy,[30] and make mistakes in his own designs. If God were truly infallible, his creations would *also* be perfect—not only spiritually but physically. For example, the

———

[29] Genesis 6:6: "And it repented the LORD that he had made man on the earth, and it grieved him at his heart."

[30] Exodus 20:5: "Thou shalt not bow down thyself to them, nor serve them: for I the LORD thy God am a jealous God, visiting the iniquity of the fathers upon the children unto the third and fourth generation of them that hate me."

human eye contains a blind spot that handicaps men and women from seeing in certain areas; the eye of the sea squid contains no such weakness. The imperfections that can be *easily* explained through evolution by natural selection *cannot* be explained by a perfect Creator—including the useless (sometimes even harmful) excess of internal organs.

These relatively common examples of "unintelligent design" help show that there *can't* be a perfect Creator God as professed by so many religious groups, including Christianity.

CONTRADICTIONS IN SCRIPTURE AND IN PRACTICES

In this chapter I will address some common problems that biblical scripture creates for itself; and because *The Bible* is supposed to be the Word of God, and therefore infallible, each contradiction leads to the eventual refutation of the Christian assumption of the authenticity and divinity of *The Bible*. Some of the inconsistencies noted in the following chapter are focused on Christianity as it was introduced in *The Bible* and how these original intents differ from modern teachings and practices—in other words, I will show that how Christianity is learned and practiced today is in many ways different than *The Holy Bible* suggests it should be, and therefore should be considered contradictory to the original teachings and tenets of the religion. Each of these disagreements is a crucial point in the disproval of Christianity as a reasonable possibility for representing true historical events because each demonstrates the fallibility of an ancient, man-written book that has been compiled and edited for thousands of years that our society has, in many ways, outgrown morally and intellectually.

• *Jesus Falsely predicts his Own Return*—Jesus Christ made various prophecies throughout the New Testament declaring foreknowledge of everything from his own death and resurrection, to his *Second Coming* and reclamation of his "Kingdom." This Second Coming revelation is well-known among Christians of all sects and denominations and is represented by various groups as the End Times, or Armageddon. There is an in-depth description of this event in the New Testament, beginning with Revelation 1:7-8: *"Behold, he cometh with clouds; and every eye shall see him, and they also which pierced him: and all kindreds of the earth shall wail because of him. Even so, Amen. I am Alpha and Omega, the beginning and the ending, saith the Lord, which is, and which was, and which is to come, the Almighty."* The problem with this prediction is that *every* generation of Christians claims that the "end is near" and many Christian groups have independently predicted specific dates for the return of their savior—all of these predictions, obviously, have failed. In fact, 52% of all those polled believe, as *The Bible* proclaims, that Jesus will return to earth someday, while 21% do not believe it. 15% believe Jesus will return *in their lifetime*; 47% do not, a *Newsweek* magazine poll reported. That same poll showed that 55% of those polled believe that every word of *The Bible* is literally accurate. 38% do not believe that about *The Bible*. The fact is, however, that Jesus himself projected his return to occur thousands of years ago. Jesus repeatedly states to his apostles that his Second Coming and the end of earth as we know it will occur *in their lifetimes*. For instance, in Matthew 24:32-34, Jesus indicates that not a generation will pass before his return and rapture: *"Now learn a parable of the fig tree; When his branch is yet tender, and putteth forth leaves, ye know that summer is nigh: So likewise ye, when ye shall see all these things, know that it is near, even at the doors. Verily I say unto you, This generation shall not pass, till all these things be fulfilled."* Many Christian apologists attempt to disregard this as an interpretive error; in other words, that the word "generation" may have been in reference to the generation of the Hebrew people, or some variation of this. Unfortunately for this argument, the Messiah's intentions are clarified in the book of Luke[31]: *"For whosoever shall be ashamed of me and of my words, of him shall the Son of man be ashamed, when he shall come in his own glory, and in his Father's, and of the holy angels. But I tell you of a truth, there be some standing here, which shall not taste of death, till they see the kingdom of God."* Jesus certainly meant that he would return while some of his followers were still living and there is no known resolution for this false prophecy put forth by Jesus.

 ◆ *One-Hundred and Twenty Years—In Genesis 6:3, The Bible* reads thusly: *"And the LORD said, My spirit shall not always strive with man, for that he also is flesh: yet his days shall be an hundred and twenty years."*[32]

This verse indicates, and most biblical scholars agree, that the Lord is limiting each human's lifespan to one hundred and twenty years of age. This is problematic for the scripture because it gives critics an exact point of comparison in which a contradiction can be created if *anyone* lives to be *more* than one hundred and twenty years old. That is a *very* long time to live, but indeed some people have surpassed the arbitrary death deadline[33]—and with advances in modern science, we expect this trend to continue. If *The Bible*

---

[31] Luke 9:26-7
[32] Genesis 6:3: "And the LORD said, My spirit shall not always strive with man, for that he also is flesh: yet his days shall be an hundred and twenty years."
[33] According to *all* surviving records, Jeanne Calment, a French woman who lived to be 122 years 164 days, has the longest lifespan in recorded history (records courtesy of Max Planck Institute for Demographic Research [MPIDR]).

explicitly indicates that man will not be able to live beyond this age, and all available records indicate that even just one person has, we are to conclude that the Christian Bible is not the infallible word of God.

A second problem with the one hundred and twenty year age limit proposed in Genesis lies within *The Bible* itself. Psalm 90:10 states very clearly that *"the days of our years are three score years and ten; and if by reason of strength they be four-score years; yet is their strength labor and sorrow; for it is soon cut off, and we fly away."* This verse is implying that man's time on earth is limited not to one hundred and twenty years, but to a maximum of eighty years. Obviously these two pieces of *The Bible* cannot be harmoniously understood in accordance with one another because they disagree explicitly. Furthermore, they are incompatible with the historical and scientific evidence of actual human lifespans.

• *Prayer versus Free Will*—the act of praying is one of the most popular practices of all Christian traditions. It is performed in church, at religious ceremonies, and at home by many Christians. It is when this prayer becomes *petitionary,* expecting God to intervene in order to achieve some result or benefit, that it becomes contradictory to the belief system built by most Christian faiths. Though *The Bible* does not mention the developed principle of "free will" explicitly, the concept dominates most of the Christian community, often as an example as to *why* there are certain types of suffering on earth. Free will refers to the God-given ability for human beings to make decisions and act without interference, whether their actions are good or bad. This is contrary to determinism, which is the belief that there is a predetermined set of events that God has already planned; this means that all of our "choices" were planned and set before we were even born, releasing all culpability from the person. If a Christian chooses to pray to their God expecting benefit for themselves or others, not only does it contradict *free will,* but the practice begins to bear a striking resemblance to the spirit conjurations of witchcraft as those who pray hope to shape and influence their perceived God's actions in a real and meaningful way.

• *God's Happiness*—assuming that God is all-knowing, all-powerful, *and* transcends time (all aspects that we are expected to believe based on modern Christian teachings in addition to biblical evidence), we can infer that God is a perfect being. If God knows all, he would know *before* earth's creation all of the pros and cons of such a creation. For example, before Adam and Eve ate from the tree that bears the fruit of the knowledge of good and evil,[34] God knew that his creations would disobey him and that he would ultimately punish them. God would also know beforehand that he would flood the earth and begin again because of man's sins, and the birth and crucifixion of Jesus would have been planned, as well. This foreknowledge would keep God from being *disappointed* in his creations, since God was already aware of what would occur before putting his plans into motion. This makes the contradicting statements in Genesis regarding God's feelings about his creations even *more* confusing: In Genesis 1:31, we see that God is satisfied with what he has built: "*And God saw every thing that he had made, and, behold, it*

———

[34] Genesis 2:7-25: "And the LORD God formed man of the dust of the ground, and breathed into his nostrils the breath of life; and man became a living soul."

was very good. And the evening and the morning were the sixth day." This is understandable, considering that a God who is perfect should create nothing but perfection. However, later in Genesis 6:6, a contradictory statement is introduced: *"And it repented the LORD that he had made man on earth, and it grieved him at his heart,"* implying that God regretted creating man after "original sin," which he had to have known would happen; not only does it not make sense for a perfect, omnipotent being to feel disappointment, but this verse implies actual *regret* as well.

• *Warrior God versus Peaceful God*—the modern teachings of Christianity often preach of a peaceful, merciful, and loving God/Creator. This is a component of the Christian tradition that is supported within the scripture of the Old and New Testaments. For example, in Romans 15:33, God is referred to as the "God of peace."[35] Culturally, this concept of a God of peace is well liked and accepted amongst clergymen and the Christian community alike; however, some scriptural evidence gives us a contradictory and seemingly destructive version of our Creator. A contradictory statement can be found in Exodus 15:3 in the description of the Lord as a "man of war."[36] In some gospels God is praised for his mercy, just judgment, and kind acts, but *The Holy Bible* also indicates another side of the *"merciful"* God. In Jeremiah 13:14,✳ *The Bible* reads: *"And I will dash them one against another, even the fathers and the sons together, saith the LORD: I will not pity, nor spare, nor have mercy, but destroy them."* This contradiction between scripture and practice is often forgotten (or ignored) in

---

[35] Romans 15:33: "Now the God of peace be with you all. Amen."
[36] Exodus 15:3: "The LORD is a man of war: The LORD is his name."

modern Christian churches, but when one honors *The Bible,* one must honor it in its entirety—including the acts of unnecessary violence that are featured within it.

✦ *Genesis and the Order of Creation*—the contradictions within the Christian Holy Scriptures begin as early as the *first* book, Genesis. In Genesis, *The Bible* outlines the creation of earth, the heavens, beasts, humanity, grass, fruit, waters, and the rest of the known world at that time in great detail with noted exclusion, of course, of the dinosaurs and other prehistoric beasts. The book of Genesis is considered to be one of the greatest pieces of *The Bible* from a literary standpoint because of its artistic components, yet the book remains problematic for the faith for reasons varying from the argument mentioned earlier in this book regarding the age of the earth (actual versus proposed age possibilities) to the various contradictions that *Genesis* creates within itself surrounding the described chronology of creation; a few of these will be listed here.

The first question that arises in Genesis is the problem of when God created *light (the Sun.)* This can be answered by two separate sections of the first chapter of the book of Genesis, which read as follows:

Genesis 1:3-5: *"And God said, Let there be light: and there was light. And God saw the light, that it was good: and God divided the light from the darkness. And God called the light Day, and the darkness he called Night. And the evening and the morning were the first day."* (Second day.)

Genesis 1:14-19: *"And God said, Let there be lights in the fir-mament of the heaven to divide the day from the night; and let them be for signs, and for seasons, and for days, and years: And let them be for lights in the firmament of the heaven to give light upon the earth: and it was so. And God made two great lights; the greater light to rule the day, and the lesser light to rule the night: he made the stars also. And God set them in the firmament of the heaven to give light upon the earth, And to rule over the day and over the night, and to divide the light from the darkness: and God saw that and it was good. And the evening and the morning were the fourth day."*

Essentially, these two passages create a confusion regarding *which* day the Sun and night were created on—the second or the fourth. Disagreements like this one are common within *The Bible* and other ancient texts, especially surrounding mythical stories, and stem from having separate manuscripts combined or compiled to create a larger text. This same contradiction is extended within Genesis to other creations such as birds, trees, other animals, and even man and woman.

Genesis 1:12: *"And the earth brought forth grass, the herb yielding seed, and the tree yielding fruit, whose seed was in itself, after his kind: and God saw that it was good."* (Plants were created before man.)

Genesis 2:4-9: *"These are the generations of the heavens and of the earth when they were created, in the day that the God made the earth and the heavens, And every plant of the field before it was in the earth, and every herb of the field before it grew: for the LORD God had not caused it to rain upon the earth, and there was not a man to till the ground. But there went up a mist from the earth, and watered the whole face of the ground. And the LORD God formed man of the dust of the ground, and breathed into his nostrils the breath of life; and man became a living soul. And the LORD God planted a garden eastward of Eden; and there he put the man whom he had formed. And out of the ground made the LORD God to grow every tree that is pleasant to the sight, and good for food; the tree of life also in the midst of the garden, and the tree of knowledge of good and evil.*" (Man was created before plants and was a necessary tool for cultivation of plant life.)

Genesis 1:27: "*So God created man in his own image, in the image of God created he him; male and female created he them.*" (Man and woman created together.)

Genesis 2:7, 21-23: "*And the LORD God formed man of the dust of the ground, and breathed into his nostrils the breath of life; and man became a living soul...And the LORD God caused a deep sleep to fall upon Adam and he slept: and he took one of his ribs, and closed up the flesh instead thereof; And the rib, which the LORD God had taken from man, made he a woman, and brought her unto the man. And Adam said, This is now bone of my bones, and flesh of my flesh: she shall be called Woman, because she was taken out of Man.*" (Woman was created sometime after man, from his rib.)

This set of Genesis verses is only a sample of the plethora of such discrepancies found in the Christian Bible. This type of contradictory language is found most often in the Gospels in which the supposed authors are relaying their versions of "actual events." When placed side by side, however, a biblical scholar is led to the conclusion that each of these stories, while clearly inspired by the same root story, omits or includes details that are crucial within the sibling texts. For example, only the canonical gospels of Matthew and Luke make mention of the supposed virgin birth of Jesus Christ, a tenet that is considered extremely important to later doctrine and modern teaching.

• *The Problem of Incest*—At various points within the Holy Scriptures, *incest* is defined as an extremely serious sin, including in Leviticus 20:17: *"And if a man shall take his sister, his father's daughter, or his mother's daughter, and see her nakedness, and she see his nakedness; it is a wicked thing; and they shall be cut off in the sight of their people: he hath uncovered his sister's nakedness; he shall bear his iniquity."* Although this quote portrays incest as "wicked," it is a common theme throughout *The Bible* and, according to Genesis, there is no other way for humanity to have begun. Adam and Eve were the only two people on earth, and they parented Cain and Abel. *The Bible* is vague in this area but does mention in Genesis 4:17 that Cain "knew his wife; and she conceived."[37] His wife would have had to come from Adam and Eve as well, making her his sister. This means that the whole of humanity was created as a product of incest, and God did not allow for any other means of reproduction, assuming that *The Bible* reports historical reality. This is not the only time that *The Bible* condones this "wicked" behavior; God also blesses Lot and his family and allows them to live when he destroys all of Sodom and Gomorrah, even though his two daughters bore their father's seed.[38] We see this recurring theme arise again when Noah and his family are forced to repopulate the earth after the flood, causing humanity to once again be

---

[37] Genesis 4:17: "And Cain knew his wife; and she conceived, and bare Enoch: and he builded a city, and called the name of the city, after the name of his son, Enoch."

[38] Genesis 19:32: "Come, let us make our father drink wine, and we will lie with him, that we may preserve seed of our father."

founded upon this *sin*. Abraham also marries his half-sister, Sarai, and receives blessings from God,[39] creating an even more contradictory teaching. If *The Bible* should be used to teach morals (the vast majority of Christians would say that it should), yet it contradicts itself on these very "moral" issues, how can it be considered the "Good Book"?

• *Divine Jesus*—Christianity attempts to reconcile Jewish monotheism and Jesus's supposed revelation as God by creating a new concept of divinity. Since the fourth century, this has been an incredibly important controversy within the Christian canon, beginning with Alexander, Arius, and the *Nicene Creed*.[40] Jesus is presented in *The Bible* as the *Son of God* and the *Son of Man* (human), but he is also taught by most modern Christian churches to be God incarnate.[41] As if this weren't enough of a contradiction—being both fully human and God simultaneously—Jesus actually separates himself from the divine God many times in *The Bible*. One example is stated in Mark 10:18: *"And Jesus said unto him, Why callest thou me good? There is none good but one, that is, God."* This self-separation is repeated throughout the Holy

---

[39] Genesis 17:15-16: "And God said unto Abraham, As for Sarai thy wife, thou shalt not call her name Sarai, but Sarah shall her name be. And I will bless her, and give thee a son also of her: yea, I will bless her, and she shall be a mother of nations; kings of people shall be of her."

[40] Nicene Creed: "And in one Lord Jesus Christ, the Son of God, begotten from the Father, only-begotten, that is, from the substance of the father, God from God, light from light, true God from true God, of one substance."

[41] John 1:1: "In the beginning there was the Word, and the Word was with God, and the Word was God" and

John 1:14: "And the Word was made flesh, and dwelt among us, and we beheld his glory, the glory as of the only begotten of the Father, full of grace and truth."

Scriptures[42] but goes against modern ideas of Jesus as an incarnation of God himself (which are especially prevalent in Catholicism and subsects of Catholic traditions.) It seems as though the evolution of Christian thought has steered the religion into a much more Jesus-centric system than it may have been originally intended by its bronze-aged creators.

• *Many Gods versus One God*—Christian orthodoxy, modern preachers, and biblical evidence would lead one to believe that there is one God, according to the Christian religion—that is the Father, Creator, the One. However, *some* books of *The Bible* seem to indicate that there are more gods. To introduce *this* series of possible biblical contradictions, I will first establish the scriptural statements that show a singular, all-powerful Lord God.

Deuteronomy 4:35: *"Unto thee it was shewed, that thou mightest know that the LORD he is God; there is none else beside him."*

1 Kings 18:39: *"The LORD, he is the God; the LORD, he is the God."*

Mark 12:32: *"There is one God; and there is none other but he."*

1 Corinthians 8:6: *"But to us there is but one God, the Father, of whom are all things, and we in him."*

These passages show a God that is much like our traditional concept of monotheistic Christian belief systems—but they are not the *whole* picture. Other biblical passages seemingly present evidence for a *plurality* of (possibly lesser) Gods present in biblical language and therefore within the Christian faith.

---

[42] Luke 22:43: "Saying, Father, if thou be willing, remove this cup from me: nevertheless not my will, but thine, be done."

Contradictions in Scripture and in Practices

Genesis 1:26: *"And God said, let us make man in our image."*

Genesis 3:22: *"And the Lord God said, Behold, then man is become as one of us, to know good and evil."*

Exodus 18:11: *"Now I know that the LORD is greater than all gods."*

Exodus 34:14: *"For thou shalt worship no other god: for the LORD, whose name is Jealous, is a jealous God."*

Deuteronomy 10:17: *"For the LORD your God is God of gods, and Lord of lords."*

Psalm 82:1: *"God standeth in the congregation of the mighty; he judgeth among the gods."*

2 Corinthians 4:4: *"In whom the god of this world hath blinded the minds of them which believe not, lest the light of the glorious gospel of Christ, who is the image of God, should shine unto them."* (Satan is the god of his world.)

A close analysis of the scripture shows *many* contradicting statements in regards to the supposed singular God that seems to dominate modern Christian thought and discourse, but it is important to note that because the books of *The Bible* were written by many different men—most unknown to us now—and in various times throughout history, it is impossible to know with certainty each individual's intent surrounding *The Bible*'s phrasing. But the fact of the matter is that the contradictory statements prove that *The Bible* cannot be the true word of a universally perfect and singular Creator.

MINOR CONTRADICTIONS

Here I will simply create a *list* of contradictions within the text of *The Holy Bible*, followed by a brief interpretation and analysis. Though I will be quoting exclusively from the Authorized King James Version, feel free to follow along in any Bible because, though wording usually varies among translations, the overall meanings are similar. Some of these are well-known, some are largely ignored, but all show that *The Bible* is false in one way or another, even if just *one* of the following is irreconcilable among the believers. Some will be differences between Old and New Testaments, some will be differences between the writings of each "apostle," and *some* of the contradictions are within the same gospel. These self-contradictions and incongruities are minor in nature, but any variation found within the text is important to note in the argument against the perpetuation of a literal understanding of Holy Scriptures within the Christian tradition, especially those that implicate larger problems within the religion.

DOES GOD TEMPT MAN?

James 1:13: *"Let no man say when he is tempted, I am tempted of God: for God cannot be tempted with evil, neither tempteth he any man."*

41

Genesis 22:1: *"And it came to pass after these things, that God did tempt Abraham, and said unto him, Abraham: and he said, Behold, here I am."*

There are various instances of "temptation" throughout the scriptures. Some are attributed to the devil, and some are attributed to God himself; yet for some reason, James 1:13 and other passages indicate that God will not tempt *any* man. This is a solid contradiction within the Holy Scriptures.

IS GOD FOREVER ANGRY?

Jeremiah 3:12: *"Go and proclaim these words toward north, and say, Return, thou backsliding Israel, saith the LORD; and I will not cause mine anger to fall upon you: for I am merciful, saith the LORD, and I will not keep anger for ever."*

Jeremiah 17:4: *"And thou, even thyself, shalt discontinue from thine heritage that I gave thee; and I will cause thee to serve thine enemies in the land which thou knowest not: for ye have kindled a fire in mine anger, which shall burn for ever."*

These passages, spaced only fourteen chapters apart in what Christians refer to as the Old Testament, conflict with each other by indicating firstly that the LORD *"will not keep anger for ever"* but shortly afterward proclaiming that *"ye have kindled a fire in mine anger, which shall burn for ever."* From this we can conclude that either the author truly did not recognize obvious disagreements in the two lines, or God changed his mind and temperament—either of which is a substantial blow to the credibility of the text.

CAN MAN SEE GOD?

John 1:18: *"No man hath seen God at any time; the only begotten Son, which is in the bosom of the Father, he hath declared him."*

Genesis 32:30: *"And Jacob called the name of the place Peniel: for I have seen God face to face, and my life is preserved."*

Exodus 33:23: *"And I [God] will take away mine hand, and thou shalt see my back parts: but my face shall not be seen."*

These are just a few lines that mention the *visibility* of God, but they create a confusing dynamic between how or if God is visually represented. In the verse from John, the author claims that "no man hath seen God at any time," yet Jacob claims to have seen God face to face in Genesis—and then in Exodus, God reveals his "back parts."

WHO WAS JOSEPH'S FATHER?

Matthew 1:16: *"And Jacob begat Joseph the husband of Mary, of whom was born Jesus, who is called Christ."*

Luke 3:23: *"And Jesus himself began to be about thirty years of age, being (as was supposed) the son of Joseph, which was the son of Heli."*

This is a well-known and controversial difference within *The Bible*; many Christians argue that the term "begat" used in Matthew 1:16 can refer to a *grandfather* as opposed to a father. Contemporary definitions and biblical context, however, show this to be untrue, as "begat" is often used in the scripture as a synonym for "fathered." This is also an important discrepancy to note because it expresses the differences that are bound to occur when related mythologies by separate authors are combined in an effort to form a seamless text.

THE PROPHECY FORETOLD THE MESSIAH WOULD BE NAMED EMMANUEL

Isaiah 7:14: *"Therefore the Lord himself shall give you a sign; Behold, a virgin shall conceive, and bear a son, and shall call his name Immanuel."*

Matthew 1:23: *"Behold, a virgin shall be with child, and shall bring forth a son, and they shall call his name Emmanuel, which being interpreted is, God with us."*

Matthew 1:24-25: *"Then Joseph being raised from sleep did as the angel of the Lord had bidden him, and took unto him his wife: And knew her not till she had brought forth her firstborn son: and he called his name JESUS."*

The prophet Isaiah *clearly* predicts that when the Christ comes to earth, he will be born of a virgin and named "Immanuel." When Jesus is born and bears a *different* name, little is discussed to address the prophetic disconnect.

DOES JESUS BRING PEACE OR A SWORD?

Matthew 10:33-34: *"But whosoever shall deny me before men, him will I also deny before my Father which is in heaven. Think not that I am come to send peace on earth: I came not to send peace, but a sword."*

John 16:33: *"These things I have spoken unto you, that in me ye might have peace. In the world ye shall have tribulation: but be of good cheer; I have overcome the world."*

There are many instances in the biblical texts in which Jesus of Nazareth condones nonviolence, and he is even referred to as the "Prince of Peace" in Isaiah.[43] But there is also a plethora of contradicting statements, such as the one indicated in Matthew 10, in which Jesus himself declares, *"I came not to send peace, but a sword."* This is also interesting to think about the "warrior god" concept introduced in an earlier chapter.

GOD DECREES THAT ADAM WILL DIE UPON CONSUMPTION OF THE FRUIT

Genesis 2:17: *"But of the tree of the knowledge of good and evil, thou shalt not eat of it: for in the day that thou eatest thereof thou shalt surely die."* (Note that if this had been the truth, humanity would not have come to fruition through Adam.)

Genesis 5:5: *"And all the days that Adam lived were nine hundred and thirty years: and he died."*

Many believers and clergymen argue that this passage indicates a different type of "death"—a spiritual death of Adam in which God would cast him out of his dominion; this does not change the fact that Adam and Eve lived *many* years after the consumption of

---

[43] Isaiah 9:6: "For unto us a child is born, unto us a son is given: and the government shall be upon his shoulder: and his name shall be called Wonderful, Counseller, The mighty God, The everlasting Father, The Prince of Peace."

the fruit and became the parents of humanity. Taken at its word, Genesis 2:17 indicates that God himself *lied* to Adam and Eve in order to keep them away from the Tree of Knowledge; it is also possible that God simply decided *not* to kill Adam as he had promised, which similarly contradicts God's supposed infallibility.

DOES GOD CHANGE HIS MIND [REPENT]?

Genesis 6:6: *"And it repented the LORD that he had made man on the earth and it grieved him at his heart."*

Numbers 23:19-20: *"God is not a man, that he should lie; neither the son of man, that he should repent: hath he said, and shall he not do it? Or hath he spoken, and shall he not make it good? Behold, I have received commandment to bless: and he hath blessed; and I cannot reverse it."*

The paradoxical aspect of an all-knowing and all-powerful God *repenting* cannot be overstated. A perfect being with omnipotence and omniscience, as described by *The Bible*, could not *create* something imperfect, let alone feel grief, repentance, or regret over having created it; yet these passages and others seem to indicate just that.

HOW MANY ANIMALS WERE TO BE SAVED BY NOAH?

Genesis 6:19-20: *"And of every living thing of all flesh, two of every sort shalt thou bring into the ark, to keep them alive with thee; they shall be male and female. Of fowls after their kind, and of cattle after their kind, of every creeping thing of the earth after his kind, two of every sort shall come unto thee, to keep them alive."*

Genesis 7:2-5: *"Of every clean beast thou shalt take to thee by sevens, the males and his female: and of beasts that are not clean by two, the male and his female. Of the fowls of the air by sevens, the male and the female; to keep see alive upon the face of all the earth. For yet seven days, and I will cause it to rain upon the earth forty days and forty nights; and every living substance that I have made will I destroy from off the face of the earth. And Noah did according unto all that the LORD commanded him."*

This is, as much of the book of Genesis and the rest of *The Bible* seems to be, riddled with contradictions. In one line, God dictates that two of each animal be saved and one chapter later Noah is instructed to take two of the *unclean* beasts and *seven* of each clean beast. In modern Christian teachings, we often only hear about God's instructions to take two of each animal. Physically, two of each animal on any size ark would be impossible to imagine as a literal truth; this is even more so the case when we see that Noah was supposedly instructed to rescue seven of each clean animal from God's Great Flood.

GOD'S FLOOD DID NOT DESTROY GIANTS?

Genesis 6:4: *"There were giants in the earth in those days; and also after that, when the sons of God came in unto the daughters of men, and they bare (sic) children to them, the same became mighty men which were of old, men of renown."* (Giants existed on earth prior to the great flood.)

Genesis 7:21: *"And all flesh died that moved upon the earth, both of fowl, and of cattle, and of beast, and of every creeping thing that creepeth upon the earth, and every man."* (All creatures except for Noah and his clan were annihilated in the flood.)

Numbers 13:33: *"And there we saw the giants, the sons of Anak, which come of the giants: and we were in our own sight as grasshoppers, and so we were in their sight."* (Giants existed on earth after the great flood.)

The statement, in Genesis, that claims that *"all flesh died that moved upon the earth"* implies just that: that all living things that weren't aboard the ark were destroyed by God's wrath. Assuming that the descendents of nephilim[44] were indeed *"in our own sight as grasshoppers, and so we were in their sight,"* we can conclude that Noah's ark could *not* fit them by sevens (or twos) in addition to the millions of other animals required to maintain their survival. This contradiction adds to the *larger* problem of the ark. Many Christians have attempted to "prove" the validity of their religion by showing the plausibility of Noah's Ark. Often this has led to modern engineers and other professionals attempting to recreate the *housing* situation within the ark. With multiples of every animal on the earth, small and large, carnivore and herbivore, predator and prey, it is hard to imagine a possible scenario in which the ark could have housed even a fraction of those animals

---

[44] Nephilim were the result of breeding between "God's sons" and humans as described in Genesis 6:1-2: "And it came to pass, when men began to multiply on the face of the earth, and daughters were born unto them, That the sons of God saw the daughters of men that they were fair; and they took them wives of all which they chose."

who exist today, and this becomes even more difficult to imagine when the giants described above enter the equation.

CAN MAN BE RIGHTEOUS?

Romans 3:10, 23: *"As it is written, There is none righteous, no, not one...For all have sinned, and come short of the glory of God."* (No man is righteous.)

Genesis 7:1: *"And the LORD said unto Noah, Come thou and all thy house into the ark; for thee have I seen righteous before me in this generation."* (Noah was righteous.)

James 5:16: *"Confess your faults one to another, and pray one for another, that ye may be healed. The effectual fervent of prayer of a righteous man availeth much."* (Prayers are effective if you are righteous.)

There are various points within *The Bible* in which God or Jesus deems one man or another as "righteous" or good, including Lot and his incestuous family, mentioned earlier. The passage in Romans 3:10, 23, however, contradicts this by stating in totality that *"There is none righteous, no, not one."*

DOES GOD DELIVER THE COMMANDMENTS UNTO MOSES THROUGH A MEDIATOR?

Exodus 20:1-17: *"And God spake all these words, saying, I am the LORD thy God which have brought thee out of the land of Egypt, out of the house of bondage. Thou shalt have no other gods before me...Thou shalt not make unto thee any graven image...Thou shalt not bow down thyself to them, nor serve them: for I the LORD thy God am a jealous God...Thou shalt not take the name of the LORD thy God in vain...Remember the Sabbath day, to keep it holy...Honour thy father and thy mother...Thou shalt not kill. Thou shalt not commit adultery. Thou shalt not steal. Thou shalt not bear false witness against thy neighbor. Thou shalt not covet thy neighbor's house, thou shalt not covet thy neighbor's wife, nor his manservant, nor his maidservant, nor his ox, nor his ass, nor any thing that is thy neighbor's."*

Galatians 3:19-20: *"Wherefore then serveth the law? It was added because of transgressions, till the seed should come to whom the promise was made; and it was ordained by angels in the hand of a mediator. Now a mediator is not a mediator of one, but God is one."*

In Exodus, there is no mention of the angelic mediator described in Galatians 3:19-20. This contradiction has been studied extensively by biblical historians and remains a mystery. Because of the mismatched accounts, it is left open to interpretation whether or not Moses actually heard God's voice in the delivery of the Ten Commandments. We can certainly say, however, that these passages cannot be reconciled and *The Bible* therefore must be fictional to some extent, and cannot be in any way considered infallible, as many Fundamentalist Christians would argue.

IS GOD ALL POWERFUL?

Revelation 19:6: *"Alleluia: For the Lord God omnipotent reigneth."* (In the Lord, anything is possible.)

Judges 1:19: "And the LORD was with Judah; and he drave out the inhabitants of the mountain; but could not drive out the inhabitants of the valley, because they had chariots of iron." (The Lord was unable to assist Judah in defeating the people of the valley because of iron chariots.)

God is described (by himself and others) throughout the biblical texts as being able to manipulate anything on earth. His all-powerful persona, however, is forgotten in *The Bible* when he fails to help Judah in defeating his enemies. This isn't the only example of God's often portrayed weaknesses, however; in fact, he must also frequently "come down" to earth in order to see certain things, meaning that he is also not omniscient.[45] God's supposed "omnipotence" is called into question throughout the Old and New Testaments when he is, to an extent, personified with human traits, emotions, flaws, and weaknesses.

It stands to reason that with God's own words showing that he simultaneously knows all that has ever happened and will ever happen *and* grieves and repents over his creations, that this in itself creates a contradiction worthy of doubt in Christianity's validity as a historical truth. Any omnipotent, omniscient, omnipresent Creator would have foreseen these problems and corrected them in advance, ensuring that the word and revelations of God would be taken seriously. Because this was not the case, we are left with written works and practices that have been altered substantially from their original state over thousands of years and today consist of various stories and "moral" teachings that often contradict one

---

[45] Genesis 11:5: "And the LORD came down to see the city and the tower, which the children of men builded."

another. As we saw in this chapter, the many biblical contradictions that the tradition creates within its own doctrine help show that *The Bible*, and the thoughts expressed throughout it, are manmade, and not divine. Because we are able to easily outline these issues—and many others—within the Christian canon, we must conclude that *The Holy Bible* and Christianity are *false* teachings and are *not* the literal Word of God.

ATROCITIES AND ABSURDITIES COMMITTED OR CONDONED BY THE LORD

"Those who can make you believe absurdities can make you commit atrocities."[46] The connection between religion and war is an aged and concrete one. Though I will not attempt to record every moment in history in which biblical evidence was cited as justification for war or slavery or worse, I *will* provide a list of atrocious and unbelievable acts committed, ordered, or rewarded by God within the Old and New Testaments. This will include rape, murder, and other seemingly *unjust* acts committed by a—supposedly—*just* God. This is necessary in order to combat those peaceful Christians who often claim that Christianity, unlike Islam, is built on the ideas of "peace" and "love". It is true that some of the biblical texts preach the importance of peaceful interactions with others, but it is equally true that our morals have evolved since these books were first written, and the acts condoned within are often brutal and barbaric. Many of the quotes below will be focused on the sadistic and malevolent acts of violence in *The Bible*, and some will be centered on biblical quotes in which acts are committed that seem *utterly absurd and ridiculous*, or otherwise improbable. In some cases, the quotes that follow may

---

[46] Voltaire, French author (1694-1778).

God doesn't stop the murder of Abel, but protects Cain?

overlap with the previous chapters on *contradictions* because God is often introduced as "loving," "caring," and "merciful."

GOD CONTROLS WHO IS MADE BLIND, DEAF, ETC.

Exodus 4:10-11: *"And Moses said unto the LORD, O my Lord, I am not eloquent, neither heretofore, nor since thou hast spoken unto thy servant: But I am slow of speech, and of a slow tongue. And the LORD said unto him, who hath made man's mouth? or who maketh the dumb, or deaf, or seeing, or the blind? have not I the LORD?"*

In the course of my studies I have discussed with Christian scholars and believers the concept of handicaps (mental and physical) being imposed on people (including children) through-out history—regardless of religious background. Many of them have claimed that it is the *devil's* work that allows babies to be born with disabilities that are no fault of their parents—and clearly no fault of their own. But this biblical passage in Exodus indicates that it is, indeed, *God* that creates these imperfections in all humans—and God that has the ability to remove them. There is no *reason* outlined (as there are no past lives taught within the Christian tradition, it cannot be punishment for sin or any variance of karma.)[47] The idea that God creates painful, difficult, and unjustified disabilities in *some* humans and not others seems arbitrary and contrary to the modern teachings of a loving Creator.

Didn't help Moses talk better, just sent Aaron.

---

[47] Karma: a cosmic principle in Hinduism and Buddhism; seen as bringing upon oneself inevitable results, good or bad, either in this life or in a reincarnation.

GOD SENDS BEARS TO MAUL FORTY-TWO CHILDREN

2 Kings 2:23-24: *"And he went up from thence unto Bethel: and as he was going up by the way, there came forth little children out of the city, and mocked him, and said unto him, Go up, thou bald head; go up, thou bald head. And he turned back, and looked on them, and cursed them in the name of the LORD. And there came forth two she bears out of the wood, and tare forty and two children of them."*

This passage is very well known in the study of biblical violence; it is a story which is often (understandably) skipped over in Sunday school, so many Christians are unaware that it exists. The narrative seems to suggest a violent God willing to justify the deaths of forty two small children for simply mocking Elisha.[48]

HUMAN BEINGS AS COMMODITIES OR PROPERTY

Exodus 21:20-21: *"And if a man smite his servant, or his maid, with a rod, and he die under his hand; he shall be surely punished. Notwithstanding, if he continue a day or two, he shall not be punished: for he is his money."*

The New International Version of *The Bible*, and others, translate this as: "If a man beats his male or female slave with a rod and the slave dies as a direct result, he must be punished." The word has been changed to servant in order to disguise the unjust acts condoned in *The Bible*. In either translation, this passage indicates that human beings can be owned and that slavery is an

---

[48] Elisha, prophet of the Hebrew Bible and disciple of Elijah.

acceptable and rewarding part of society. However, this is but *one* of the passages in *The Holy Bible* that condones and/or regulates the ownership of human beings, Leviticus has various examples as well.[49]

MOSES TO HIS SOLDIERS

Numbers 31:17-18: *"Now therefore kill every male among the little ones, and kill every woman that hath known man by lying with him. But all the women children, that have not known a man by lying with him, keep alive for yourselves."*

The "spoils of war" mentioned by Moses in this passage are a brutal reminder of the time period in which the stories of *The Bible* were written; women and children being captured as slaves (for sex *and* labor) at various points in the texts, even by supposedly righteous men, such as Moses.

LOT[50] AND INCEST

Genesis 19:31-36: *"And the firstborn said unto the younger, Our father is old, and there is not a man in the earth to come in unto us after the manner of all the earth: Come, let us make our father drink wine, and we will lie with him, that we may preserve seed of our father. And they made their father drink wine that night: and the*

---

[49] Genesis 17:13, Exodus 21:20-21, Leviticus 25:44-46, Deuteronomy 21:10-14, etc.
[50] Lot was the nephew of the patriarch Abraham, or Abram. He was the son of Abraham's brother Haran (Gen. 11:27).

firstborn went in, and lay with her father; and he perceived not when she lay down, nor when she arose. And it came to pass on the morrow, that the firstborn said unto the younger, Behold, I lay yesternight with my father: let us make him drink wine this night also; and go thou in, and lie with him, that we may preserve seed of our Father. And they made their father drink wine that night also: and the younger arose, and lay with him; and he perceived not when she lay down, nor when she arose. Thus were both the daughters of Lot with child by their father."

2 Peter 2:7-8: *"And delivered just Lot, vexed with the filthy conversation of the wicked (For that righteous man dwelling among them, in seeing and hearing, vexed his righteous soul from day to day with their unlawful deeds)."* (Lot characterized as just and righteous.)

Lot is a crucial character in various texts throughout the Holy Scriptures... but much can be said about his various sins and subsequent designation as a "righteous man." The above passage of Lot and his *loving* daughters is one of the most well-known narratives featuring him and his family and was discussed in previous chapters; the lesser-known stories, however, are much more controversial. Lot is also featured in Genesis 19:5-8[51] in which he attempts to convince the Sodomites to take his two "virgin" daughters as sexual objects as opposed to the angels that

---

[51] Genesis 19:5-8: "And they called unto Lot, and said unto him, Where are the men which came in to thee this night? Bring them out unto us, that we may know them. And Lot went out at the door unto them, and shut the door after them, And said, I pray you, brethren, do not so wickedly. Behold now, I have two daughters which have not known man; let me, I pray you, bring them out unto you, and do ye to them as is good in your eyes: only unto these men do nothing; for therefore came they under the shadow of my roof."

he is housing. This act is deemed pious by his God, and Lot is spared during the destruction of Sodom and Gomorrah, though his wife was turned into a "pillar of salt"[52] for "looking back"—a seemingly unjustifiable punishment, when he and his incest-committing children were left to live. It is interesting to note that Lot and his family are continually deemed righteous by God throughout the Old Testament in spite of the instances of incest, allowed rape, etc. noted above.

A Rich Man Shall Hardly Enter Heaven

Matthew 19:20-24: *"The young man saith unto him, All these things have I kept from my youth up: what lack I yet? Jesus said unto him, If thou wilt be perfect, go and sell that thou hast, and give to the poor, and thou shalt have treasure in heaven: and come follow me. But when the young man heard that saying, he went away sorrowful: for he had great possessions. Then Jesus said unto his disciples, Verily I say unto you, that a rich man shall hardly enter into the kingdom of heaven. And again I say unto you, It is easier for a camel to go through the eye of a needle, than for a rich man to enter the kingdom of God."*

This passage in the book of Matthew tells the story of a dialogue between a young man and Jesus of Nazareth. During the

—

[52] Genesis 19:23-26: "The sun was risen upon the earth when Lot entered into Zoar. Then the LORD rained upon Sodom and upon Gomorrah brimstone and fire from the LORD out of heaven; And he overthrew those cities and all the plain, and all the inhabitants of the cities, and that which grew upon the ground. But his wife looked back from behind him, and she became a pillar of salt."

interaction, the young man asks Jesus how he may become perfect and righteous in the eyes of God. Jesus responds by telling the individual that he must first give up all of his worldly possessions in exchange for an ascetic lifestyle following the teachings of the Christ; this is not an unfamiliar concept and is found in various religions. After the supposedly wealthy man walks away from the offer, Jesus tells his disciples that "it is easier for a camel to go through the eye of a needle, than for a rich man to enter the kingdom of God," indicating that poverty or destitution is an *additional* requirement for acceptance into heaven and therefore eternal bliss in communion with God. This is a principle that is taught by Jesus and is rarely observed in the modern Christian lay community, though some monastic Christians still participate in the puritanical tradition taught in *The Bible*. Those Christians who both believe that the words of Jesus Christ (and *The Bible*) are the truth of God *and* also have worldly possessions must also acknowledge that it is easier for a camel to fit in the eye of a needle than for them to be accepted into heaven by Jesus Christ. The teaching has merit in its intent, which is to encourage charitable behavior. It is the fact that this concept of Christian morality has been left behind in modern practitioners that makes this a valid point for an argument *against* the Christian dogma.

FIRE AND BRIMSTONE FROM HEAVEN?

Genesis 19:23-26: *"The sun was risen upon the earth when Lot entered into Zoar. Then the LORD rained upon Sodom and upon Gomorrah brimstone and fire from the LORD out of heaven; And he overthrew those cities and all the plain, and all the inhabitants of the cities, and that which grew upon the ground. But his wife looked back from behind him, and she became a pillar of salt."*

Traditional Christian views of heaven paint the picture of a luxurious oasis in the clouds in which worldly worries and concerns have no place. This quote, however, illustrates the Lord raining "brimstone and fire from the Lord out of heaven"—indicating that contemporary ideas of heaven and hell may be different from what *The Bible* actually teaches. This passage is also unique because, in addition to challenging the popular views of the Christian heaven, it also shows the cruel punishments bestowed upon humanity by the Lord for something as trivial as "looking back from behind him"... for which the Lord felt it necessary to transform her into a pillar of salt. Christians fail to acknowledge heaven as a place where violence could occur but, judging by this passage and others (especially in the Old Testament), it is hard to imagine that there could be *peace* in communion with the Judeo-Christian God.

THE LORD SLAYS THE ETHIOPIANS

Zephaniah 2:11-13: *"The LORD will be terrible unto them: for he will famish all the gods of earth; and men shall worship him, every one from his place, even all the isles of the heathen. Ye Ethiopians also, ye shall be slain by my sword. And he will stretch out his hand against the north, and destroy Assyria; and will make Nineveh a desolation, and dry like a wilderness."*

This quote is relatively self-explanatory, but it does demonstrate how the Lord punishes some humans even *before* death. In this instance, all Ethiopians were to be destroyed, but this is only one occasion in which God's terrible wrath is invoked on humankind. This is a commonly cited example of God's cruelty—but not the only one.

BREAKING THE SABBATH PUNISHABLE BY DEATH

Exodus 31:14: *"Ye shall keep the Sabbath therefore; for it is holy unto you: every one that defileth it shall surely be put to death: for whosoever doeth any work therein, that soul shall be cut off from among his people."*

The holy day, in Christianity, is Sunday, or the Sabbath. This is the seventh day, on which God was said to have rested after his creation of the earth. This quote from Exodus describes that if one *"doeth any work"* or *"defileth"* this day, he or she shall bring God's judgment upon himself or herself *during this lifetime*. While this biblical law was largely observed for years after *The Bible*'s creation and is still taken seriously by some fringe religious groups, especially Orthodox Jews, it is no longer thought by the majority of believers to be a binding law. The remnants of this idea, however, are still apparent in American society with the closure of some stores and governmental offices on Sundays. This does not change the fact that *most* people who consider themselves "Christians" treat the supposedly holy day as any other, especially in terms of doing physical activity or manual labor.

Was he high?

✳ The Resurrected "Armies" of Bones

Ezekiel 37:1-14: *"The hand of the LORD was upon me, and carried me out in the spirit of the LORD, and set me down in the midst of the valley which was full of bones, And caused me to pass by them round about: and, behold, there were very many in the open valley; and, lo, they were very dry. And he said unto me, Son of man, can these bones live? And I answered, O Lord GOD, thou knowest. Again he said unto me, Prophesy upon these bones, and say unto them, O ye dry bones, hear the word of the LORD. Thus saith the Lord GOD unto these bones; Behold I will cause breath to enter into you, and ye shall live: And I will lay sinews upon you, and will bring up flesh upon you, and cover you with skin, and put breath in you, and ye shall live; and ye shall know that I am the LORD. So I prophesied, there was a noise, and behold a shaking, and the bones came together, bone to his bone. And when I beheld, lo, the sinews and the flesh came up upon them, and the skin covered them above: but there was no breath in them. Then said he unto me, Prophesy unto the wind, prophesy, son of man, and say to the wind, Thus saith the Lord GOD; Come from the four winds, O breath, and breathe upon these slain, that they may live. So I prophesied as he commanded me, and the breath came into them, and they lived, and stood upon their feet, an exceeding great army. Then he said unto me, Son of man, these bones are the whole house of Israel: behold, they say, Our bones are dried, and our hope is lost: we are cut off for our parts. Therefore prophesy and say unto them, thus saith the Lord GOD; Behold, O my people, I will open your graves, and cause you to come up out of your graves, and bring you into the land of Israel. And ye shall know that I am the LORD, when I have opened your graves, O my people, and brought you up out of your graves, And shall put my spirit in you, and ye shall live, and I shall place you in your own land: then shall ye know that I the LORD have spoken it, and performed it, saith the LORD."*

This quote, from the book of Ezekiel, describes a well-known prophecy amongst the Judeo-Christian religionists in which armies of men are raised from the grave and given life through the power of the Lord. This is considered to be an extremely absurd and radical idea, to say the least.

HATE THY FATHER AND THY MOTHER

Luke 14:26: *"If any man come to me, and hate not his father, and mother, and wife, and children, and brethren, and sisters, yea, and his own life also, he cannot be my disciple."*

In this passage, Jesus explains the prerequisites for becoming his follower and disciple. Jesus, the Christ, Messiah, and "Son of Man" does, in fact, say that hatred for one's family is necessary before becoming his follower. This is contradictory to the Judeo-Christian idea of the Ten Commandments, of which *"Honor thy father and thy mother"* is a central principle, but it is not hard to understand why Jesus would say this. In fact, Jesus praises ignorance and separateness from loved ones throughout the texts; this is a fact that even the most liberal Christian scholars cannot disagree with. The reason for this is simple: cult mentality. In order to cultivate a group of people who will dedicate their lives to you, or to God, or to anything, they must first be alienated from this world. Jesus and Christianity did not invent this concept, and will not be the last to use it as a conversion tactic. It's unfortunate, however, that modern Christians are often unable to recognize this.

The Subservience of Women

Genesis 3:16-17: *"Unto the woman he said, I will greatly multiply thy sorrow and thy conception; in sorrow thou shalt bring forth children; and thy desire shall be to thy husband, and he shall rule over thee. And unto Adam he said, Because thou has hearkened unto the voice of thy wife, and hast eaten of the tree, of which I commanded thee, saying, Thou shalt not eat of it: cursed is the ground for thy sake; in sorrow shalt thou eat of it all the days of thy life."*

Because Eve was the bearer of "original sin" by first eating from the Tree of Knowledge, God ensures that she and all of her female descendents will pay for the trespass by enduring painful childbirth and being ruled by man. This concept causes me to ask the question "what about animal birth?" Why do *many* animals suffer through labor if they did not participate in original sin? And, furthermore, if Eve had chosen *not* to disobey God, would she bear children without pain? This idea of "bringing forth children" in sorrow is a complicated one, and is not elaborated upon much further in the text. It does leave the reader wondering how God expected Eve to procreate without pain—and why animals already knew the pains of childbirth. This is another verse rarely discussed in churches in the modern Christian faiths, primarily because the idea of man as master of his woman is no longer socially accepted; yet this passage clearly enforces the idea of the subservience of women by dictating that *"thy desire shall be to thy husband, and he shall rule over thee.* "The designation of this idea by many as amoral or primitive reinforces the fact that *The Bible* is a fixed, stagnant, man-made, compilation; as our morality evolves and we learn about social equality, *The Bible* remains steadfast against it.

GOD'S CONDEMNATION OF SHRIMP AND SHELLFISH

Leviticus 11:9-12: *"These shall ye eat of all that are in the waters: whatsoever hath fins and scales in the waters, in the seas, and in the rivers, them shall ye eat. And all that have not fins and scales in the seas, and in the rivers, of all that move in the waters, and of any living thing which is in the waters, they shall be an abomination unto you: They shall be even an abomination onto you; ye shall not eat of their flesh, but ye shall have their carcasses in abomination. Whatsoever hath no fins nor scales in the waters, that shall be an abomination unto you."*

Only a few chapters before God's condemnation of homosexuality,[53] the Lord decrees that the consumption of water-dwelling animals *without* fins and scales is an abomination (including shrimp, shellfish, water mammals, etc.). This strong language, the same terms used in reference to homosexuals, demonstrates the seriousness of the Christian damnation thought to occur as a result of eating these animals. This passage and its repercussions are largely forgotten or ignored in the teachings of modern Christianity, though its equivalent regarding the "abomination" of homosexuality continues to be a dominant idea in

---

[53] Leviticus 18:22. See page 14 above for detailed quote and analysis.

Christian thought. The Christian Bible is composed of the Old *and* New Testaments, yet the holy laws taught in Genesis and Leviticus are often downplayed and/or forgotten, when convenient, of course. In this case, the consumption of water-dwelling animals other than fish is portrayed as a hell-worthy offense, yet many Christians remain ignorant or simply uncaring in regards to the sinful transgressions of eating these animals. This contradiction has caused some non-believing activists to satirically carry signs saying "God Hates Shrimp"—mocking the hateful "God Hates Fags" signs made popular by the Westboro Baptist Church, led by Fred Phelps.

LET YOUR WOMEN KEEP SILENCE

1 Corinthians 14:34-35: *"Let your women keep silence in the churches: for it is not permitted unto them to speak; but they are commanded to be under obedience, as also saith the law. And if they will learn any thing, let them ask their husbands at home: for it is a shame for women to speak in the church."*

Bible verses are often used as wedding vows throughout the Christian and even non-Christian world, and one of the most popular passages quoted for this purpose is 1 Corinthians 13:4-13. It may sound most familiar in the more commonly recited translation of the New International Version: *"Love is patient, love is kind. It does not envy, it does not boast, it is not proud. It is not rude, it is not self-seeking, it is not easily angered, it keeps no record of wrongs. Love does not delight in evil but rejoices with the truth. It always protects, always trusts, always hopes, always perseveres. And now faith, hope, and love abide, but the greatest of these is love."* This verse is a beautiful piece of scriptural literature that sometimes helps people demonstrate their commitment to one another; less than one entire chapter following this widespread passage however, the intolerant and sexist portion of 1 Corinthians begins and regulates the speech of women. The irony in this is largely ignored in modern society, partially because of the fact that this portion of the book of Corinthians isn't taught in many churches—as is the case with many controversial sections of *The Holy Bible.*

JEALOUS AND FURIOUS LORD CAUSES NATURAL DISASTERS

Nahum 1:2-6: *"God is jealous, and the LORD revengeth; the LORD revengeth, and is furious; the LORD will take vengeance on his adversaries, and he reserveth wrath for his enemies. The LORD is slow to anger, and great in power, and will not at all acquit the wicked: the LORD hath his way in the whirlwind and in the storm, and the clouds are dust of his feet. He rebuketh the sea, and maketh it dry, and drieth up all the rivers: Bashan languisheth, and Carmel, and the flower of Lebanon languisheth. The mountains quake at him, and the hills melt, and the earth is burned at his presence, yea, the world, and all that dwell therein. Who can stand before his indignation? And who can abide in the fierceness of his anger? His fury is poured out like fire, and the rocks are thrown down by him."*

The term "acts of God" is often used to describe a natural disaster... but few people consider why these unnecessary and deadly catastrophes occur on earth every day.[54] Pious people, Christians, Muslims, Atheists, Jews, every sect of humanity can perish in earthquakes, volcanic eruptions, hurricanes, and more with *no* human intervention—and as *The Bible* says, *"The Lord hath his way in the whirlwind and in the storm, and the clouds are dust of his feet... The mountains quake at him, and the hills melt, and the earth is burned at his presence... His fury is poured out like fire, and the rocks are thrown down by him."* This brings to mind the "explanatory context" in which most gods are introduced into society; from the sun gods, war gods, thunder gods, earth gods, and water gods of Greek mythology and many other traditions to the all-encompassing God of Christian mythology. Human beings will always seek to explain the things that they do not understand; throughout the history of mankind, the invention of god(s) was often the most reasonable solution. But the Judeo-Christian God is without a doubt the cause of natural disasters, according to *The Bible*. And there is no reasonable explanation for these atrocities; the Christian response is to simply designate these as "parts of God's greater plan."

These various injustices and carnal acts perpetrated and accepted by the ancient Christian and Hebrew God prove that even the argument that *The Holy Bible* is *not* meant to be taken literally (an idea that we have already disproven with scripture), but instead as a moral guide sent by God, is also *false*. While the justifications for murder, slavery, war, rape, and hatred of fellow man *would* have been acceptable to those living in the time period in which it is

---

[54] For more information on the "Natural Disaster Argument", see page 27 for a detailed analysis

written, today the followers of the Christian tradition attempt to pick and choose which words to live by—and they forget the terrible acts that their God has committed and will continue to commit, according to dogma. The act of exclusion of *some* biblical aspects and acceptance of others demonstrates that the words of *The Holy Bible* are *not* time-transcendent and, as humanity evolves, our morals and principles evolve with us.

CONCLUSION

As illustrated by the previous chapters, it is impossible to argue that *The Holy Bible* (which is presupposed by *The Bible* itself *and* the majority of Christian theologians, including the Roman Catholic papal community, to be *infallible*) is without faults once you are well informed in regards to its contents. Many people, as I have discovered throughout the course of my studies, have no qualms with labeling themselves or their *children* as Christians without extensive self-investigation into the holy texts or even some of the practiced beliefs of the tradition in modern context. We have analyzed contradictions and arguments that prove that the words of *The Holy Bible*, and therefore the teachings of the Christian community, *cannot* be a representation of an omnipotent Creator. This is not to say that any other religion is *more* "true" than the Judeo-Christian sects, but we simply began with Christianity as a starting point in order to show the little-known facts and seldom-followed biblical laws of the most popular religion in the world.

Even if a believer chooses to discount *The Bible* as a figurative or imaginative representation of a true God and Jesus Christ, which is of course contrary to the biblical evidence and evangelical/orthodox Christian teachings, the *"Atrocities and Absurdities Committed or Condoned by the Lord"* chapter of the book demonstrates that *The Bible* may have been useful as a literary guide to morality at some point, but in a modern society in which rape, slavery, incest, and murder are no longer acceptable, it is an archaic book, based on very little historical evidence and teaching irrelevant and archaic principles to its adherents.

My book was not written in hate for Christians or distain for the principles often associated with Jesus Christ—instead it was inspired by the ignorance that faith and religion often breed in humanity; the type of ignorance that allows a person to self-identify as a Christian (or any other religion) without having first researched the Holy Scriptures themselves in order to properly evaluate the religion's veracity or falsity.

My sincere hope is that the quotes and arguments presented in this pocket guide to the refutation of Christianity resonate with its readers, Christian or not, because of the valid points that they raise in regards to the validity (or lack thereof) of monotheism, Christianity, Judaism, and other monotheistic traditions. In order to *believe* in something, it is my assertion that first one must properly *understand* it; in the case of Christianity, this consists of a strong knowledge of Christian history, modern teachings, *and* biblical lessons in context—which many modern Christians lack.

PART TWO

OTHER SECULAR ESSAYS

THERE ARE NO SACRIFICES FOR THE OMNIPOTENT: THE JESUS CONTRADICTION

A common theme throughout the New Testament scriptures *and* modern teachings of Christianity is that of "personal sacrifice." Whether a parable in *The Bible* is teaching the disciples and followers of Jesus how to sacrifice themselves for the Lord, or to live without worldly riches in order to be more like Jesus, self-sacrifice is a common tenet of *all* sects of Christianity—and many other religions for that matter. The act that comes to mind more often than any other in a Christian context is Jesus' crucifixion—the ultimate act of self-sacrifice that forgave mankind's sins and makes future flesh donations to God unnecessary; or so it is taught by the Christian dogma.

The question that arises in my mind, when prompted with this idea of Jesus' ultimate sacrifice, involves the omnipotence and omniscience of God. If we presuppose that Jesus and God are one—as many (but not all) Christians do—then we can also infer that Jesus Christ was omnipotent, omniscient, and omni-benevolent, and it is with this that the idea of *sacrifice* is lost. The martyrdom was premeditated on the part of the Creator, and Jesus was resurrected afterward—showing that the act of "death" was not an inconvenience for the immortal "man" who was said to have *known* that he would be resurrected. It is because of this that these acts lack the sacrificial element that is often praised through-out modern Christianity.

A Glitch in God's System: The Paradox of Divine Intervention

The science and psychology of religion boils down to a few, main pillars: faith, uniformed beliefs, and fear of the unknown. But regardless of which tradition you subscribe to, it is composed of many divine doctrinal assertions. A popular theological assertion, especially common among monotheistic traditions is that a Higher Power, or "God", controls aspects of their daily lives and gives punishment and reward based on good and bad behavior. For instance, you may hear a singer on television thanking "God" for the success of their most recent album, or see untimely deaths justified with "God's Plan". I was recently confronted, in the form of a hostile e-mail, by the claim that God might punish me for my secular writings and lifestyle *in this lifetime*. This idea prompted me to examine my life in search of these divine consequences.

I explored my school, work, and home lives and quickly came to the realization that there must be a glitch in God's system. I have somehow avoided his wrath of punishment that I should be subjected to for my essays and my beliefs (or lack thereof) in general. I pondered how content I was with my life and concluded that the small instances of random misfortunes are statistically rare and insignificant—and not to be *blamed* on an unknowable deity. I have a happy, healthy, loving family and I do what I love... In fact, I would argue that I am happier with my life than the average believer. For example, if I have a loved one who doesn't honor the *same* religion as me, I don't worry about the possibility of them being sentenced to eternal damnation in hellfire for their "sins", as some modern religions would warrant. I have an open mind that, history shows us, could be significantly restricted if I adhered to a specific religion—trying to fit all that I learn within an established paradigm of a single tradition is impossible; yet so many attempt it for the sake of feeling more comfortable with the unknown or for cultural assimilation. I find comfort in my beliefs being founded in science—and not faith; I can live my life by my own, instinctual, human morals and not worry about what a "God" might think and what type of punishment that I may or may not receive. Overall, I've learned that I cannot fathom a way in which the presence of a "god figure" in my life would improve it.

A LETTER TO THE CHRISTIAN HYPOCRITES

For all of the "Christians" who...

...don't abide by the dietary laws of Leviticus...

Leviticus 11:9-12: *"These shall ye eat of all that are in the waters: whatsoever hath fins and scales in the waters, in the seas, and in the rivers, them shall ye eat. And all that have not fins and scales in the seas, and in the rivers, of all that move in the waters, and of any living thing which is in the waters, they shall be an abomination unto you: They shall be even an abomination onto you; ye shall not eat of their flesh, but ye shall have their carcases in abomination. Whatsoever hath no fins nor scales in the waters, that shall be an abomination unto you."*

...didn't save their virginity for marriage, work on the Sabbath...

Exodus 31:14: *"Ye shall keep the Sabbath therefore; for it is holy unto you: every one that defileth it shall surely be put to death: for whosoever doeth any work therein, that soul shall be cut off from among his people."*

...and have accumulated worldly wealth...

Matthew 19:20-24: *"The young man saith unto him, All these things have I kept from my youth up: what lack I yet? Jesus said unto him, If thou wilt be perfect, go and sell that thou hast, and give to the poor, and thou shalt have treasure in heaven: and come follow me. But when the young man heard that saying, he went away sorrowful: for he had great possessions. Then Jesus said unto his disciples, Verily I say unto you, that a rich man shall hardly enter into the kingdom of heaven. And again I say unto you, It is easier for a camel to go through the eye of a needle, than for a rich man to enter the kingdom of God."*

...I ask *why* you would label yourself as a follower of an outdated tradition that you do *not* understand.

All that I ask is that you question the beliefs that were (most likely) implanted in your mind as a young child and *hopefully* research your so-called holy texts. If you read *The Bible* from a modern and intellectual perspective, I doubt that you will have the spiritual experience that you might expect if you are used to listening to well-rehearsed sermons. Instead, you will be disgusted with your God and most likely find the archaic principles the book teaches lacking modern relevance and scientific evidence.

According to your holy book, every single Buddhist, Jew, Hindu, Muslim, follower of various minor traditions or sects, those who do not affiliate themselves with a religious tradition and the approximately 2.74 billion humans who have never had the "privilege" of hearing the word of your Messiah[55] will be sentenced to eternal damnation in a lake of fire—regardless of moral standings or positive worldly accomplishments. If this sounds like a fair proposition to you, then I bite my tongue—but I honestly believe that the majority of Christians do *not* agree with these doctrinal assertions, and instead categorize themselves as "Christians" out of cultural familiarity or perhaps out of complete ignorance in regards to the topic.

---

[55] Statistics according to "The Joshua Project" global mission statistics.

I have always been in awe of those people who consider themselves followers and messengers of Christ and know little to nothing about the history, origins, beliefs, or tenets of the tradition—but for *those* Christians, it is important to acknowledge that a WWJD bracelet and a "Jesus Loves You" bumper sticker do not make you *pious*. And researching a topic before devoting your life to its assumptions does not make you a sinner or a bad person, it means that you are using the tools at your disposal to make an informed, spiritual, decision; there is no harm in studying the belief system on which you are risking your supposed afterlife, and I'm sure any *all-knowing* deity would agree.

WHY ATHEISTS SHOULD UNDERSTAND THE BIBLE

Religionists have two primary ways of spreading doctrine: *heredity* (the passing of religious customs from generation to generation) and *formal outward conversion* (door-to-door and conversational *peddling* of religion). Regardless of *which* religion is being practiced, there are various cited cases of conversion *and* indoctrination of men, women, and most crucially, children. It is clear, however, that the latter is a more effective tactic in the expansion of a belief system. Each religion (at least all successful ones) has a built-in form of reward and punishment system that ensures, to a high probability, that the beliefs and practices are passed successfully from parent to child. After all, a parent who believes that punishment for disbelief is damnation will do anything in their power to ensure that their children *do* believe.

In order to think about this phenomenon in practical terms, I apply the analogy of Santa Claus. I am not necessarily equating the idea of a "God" to a jolly, Christmas, caricature—but it *is* interesting to note that *many* families raise their children by enforcing a belief in Santa Claus. And if nobody ever told the child that he *doesn't* exist, it is reasonable to conclude that many children would mature and maintain the belief in Saint Nicolas and possibly raise their children with those same beliefs and so on and so forth, continuing the practices associated with the benevolent gift-giver and his holiday. This is *exactly* what we see with religion.

It is because of this "gift" of faith that most religionists (often in accordance with their respective doctrines) raise their children to mirror their own religious ideologies and transform the blank slates that are their children into followers of a system which they rarely question, these culturally-indoctrinated Christians often neglect to follow the basic tenets and principles of the faith. There is one major flaw in this technique employed by virtually every religion in the world—and that is that, in order for a theistic system to spread and remain relevant—it depends on *faith*, in other words "ignorance". This is often at the opposition of common sense and scientific facts. I've found that, through the spread of knowledge and reason, it is possible to combat faith-based theism on an individual basis, but it is also extremely difficult. Some people become so set in these beliefs that it is impossible for them to fathom another reality.

I'm not saying that it is an easy task to "deconvert" or even hold a logical dialogue with *some* religionists; after all, in many cases, they have devoted their entire lives to honoring and revering their "God(s)". There are, however, many people who are both intelligent and reasonable, yet they have never questioned their inherited theistic traditions—*these people I refer to as "religious by default". While, if asked, they would likely classify themselves as "believers" or "followers"—they may not strictly follow, or even be fully aware, of the basic tenets of their religion.* In North America (and Europe), the "default religion" is usually a sect of Christianity, this is important because these softer *Default Christians*, as opposed to evangelical, fundamentalist, and extremist Christians, make up the (silent) majority. It is upon this realization that I suggest a "Secular Surge", on behalf of non-theists around the world, in order to spread logical thinking and knowledge at the expense of blind faith—in order to ensure that science, society, and government are no longer impacted and restrained by the archaic pillars upon which supernatural religions, cults, and theism in general are built.

In order to have *any* hope of accomplishing such an incredible task, it is first necessary for the secularists and non-religious people to become well-informed in that which they will attempt to refute—this includes taking Religious Studies courses, attending a church or other religious institution, or even a close-reading of the canonical Sacred Texts. *I write this in response to the many e-mails I have received on why I focus so much of my time studying traditions that I believe to be false and often harmful.* I believe that, as a secular activist and Religious Studies graduate, it is often helpful to know more about the religions that I spend my time denouncing than the majority of its followers.

RELIGION AND WAR:
THE CHICKEN AND THE EGG

Religionists often misinterpret my (and other atheist activists') assertions regarding the close relationship between war and religion; this is a problem that the secular community has often faced—and one that I will now attempt to rectify. The idea, in particular, that I wish to address is the strong and apparent link between *all* popular religions and violence, murder, and war. You may have heard the popular argument *against* religion that, in one way or another, suggests that religion is uniquely dangerous because it *causes* war. This concept can be *easily* refuted by any thinking person by simply calling to attention the fact that wars existed prior to religion—and humans will continue to wage war long after the reign of religion.

It's not necessarily that religion *causes* brutality and war—but that it *justifies* acts that, otherwise, would be considered unacceptable. But religion, theism, and spirituality aren't the *only* mind-altering constructions within humanity that have spawned dangerous ideas; nationalism, for example, has a similar effect on people. It is the "blind faith" that these two institutions often create in individuals and groups that has caused many of the world's largest violent disputes and issues. Legitimizing the practice of basing ideas and actions on matters that cannot be proved can result in some very unfortunate consequences. The habit of accepting things on faith can lead an otherwise rational person to follow the orders of extremists without giving due consideration to the impact and consequences which these actions might have for themselves and for others.

When this concept of religious or "holy" war is discussed in modern, western, society—the conversation often drifts towards Islamic issues of Jihad—but an enormous amount of earthly historic wars were caused or perpetuated by Christian leaders and believers. In fact, Christianity can be traced to the roots of many of today's most recognizable wars and injustices; from the Christian Crusades, to the formation of the Ku Klux Klan, to Hitler's genocidal master plan, to the imperialist colonization of America—this violent aspect of Christianity is *radically* embedded in its past, present, and future.

In conclusion, the key word when discussing religion and its many complicated ties to war is "justification." In many cases, using religion to justify a specific violent act allows other followers of that religion to declare that act "righteous"—regardless of the consequences, victims, and ulterior motives. If you are religious, you believe that your religion is the "right" one—and, in many cases, all others will be sent to hell. Similarly, a nationalist believes his or her nation is better or more advanced—and a *racist* believes that an inherent difference between each race make his or her ethnicity superior. *All* of these ideologies spawn the hate, philosophical disagreements, and prejudices that have been the catalysts for various atrocious acts throughout history.

Two Nations, Under God: The Canadian Charter from an American Perspective

As an American scholar of *Religious Studies*—as opposed to Theology—I am accustomed to studying religions and their various effects on society (positive *and* negative) from an *objective* point of view. I look at religion from a phenomenological approach and analyze how it came to be, why people continue to practice these ancient traditions, and what similarities each religion holds to one another. In American society, I particularly focus on the hypocrisy of the term *"separation of church and state"*—and how it holds little meaning in the American culture in which "IN GOD WE TRUST" is printed on all legal tender, and churches participating in political actions remain tax-exempt. From the pledge of allegiance, to the very laws we live by, religion (specifically Christianity) is sewn into the fabrics of America's past, present, and future.

The reason I tend to focus on The United States of America (other than that it happens to be the nation of my birth) is its unique place in the religious community; the USA is able to claim separation of church and state as a founding principle of the nation while creating laws and governmental ideas that are distinctly contrary to that very idea. This is different from nations that are either openly theocratic in nature or have a truly secular government. Canada, for example, is much more secular in nature—with the most recent government census surveys indicating that nearly 17% of Canadian citizens claim to be affiliated with *no* religion[56] compared to a miniscule 11-14% in America. It wasn't until recently, however, that it was brought to my attention that the Canadian *government* actually recognizes a God. Though the United States of America is a highly Christian nation and it is obvious in our federal and state governments, our constitution remains a *secular* document that respects the right of all peoples to practice any or no religion; not all nations have this luxury.

Much like the Pledge of Allegiance in America, the Canadian anthem ("O, Canada") was originally created *without* any religious acknowledgements or undertones. The official Canadian National Anthem, written in 1880, had no mention of a "God" in its original lyrics; through revisions and translations, however, the words "God keep our land glorious and free!" were placed in the anthem and have remained there since an *official* Act of Parliament was signed into law making "O, Canada" the country's national anthem in 1980. The history of the Canadian anthem is strikingly similar to that of the American pledge of allegiance. The religious nature of "O, Canada", though recognized by the federal government as a national anthem, is *not* unique to Canada in that it is not built into the actual constitution—it is simply an anthem for the nation. This is where the similarities end between the American and Canadian governmental recognition and acceptance of a God.

---

[56] Statistics   Canada,   Census   of   Population   2005. http://www40.statcan.ca/l01/cst01/demo30a-eng.htm

As you may already know, the country of Canada features another approach to the supernatural that is governmental in nature. In addition to the anthem, the Canadian government also supports a preamble to the Canadian Constitution (or Charter)—that is universally accepted by the Canadian government as a document that guides the nation's laws and constitutional guarantees—and recognizes Canadian subservience to a higher power. The preamble of the Canadian Charter states "Whereas Canada is founded upon principles that recognize the supremacy of God and the rule of law" which indicates the Canadian allegiance to "God" and, because of this Charter provision, Canada is not necessarily guaranteed any secular liberties. This enables Canadian federal government to have the fluidity between government and church that the United States Constitution (in theory) does *not*.

This fact regarding the presence of "God" in the preamble of the Canadian Charter, though clearly well-known throughout the Canadian provinces, comes as a surprise to many secular activists in America and other nations who are used to a more subtle bridge between church and state. Because of this theism-laced political system in Canada, citizens (regardless of religious affiliation) are forced to endure not only the singing of a theist-based national song, but also Christian prayers before various federal events—including meetings for the creation of legislation. It is surprising to learn that though the *people* of Canada are less likely to be affiliated with a religious tradition than those in America, the *governing body* itself, in Canada, has a recognized deity that allows for the trampling of the rights to religious freedom of anybody who does *not* recognize the monotheistic Judeo-Christian God.

About the Author

David G. McAfee is a journalist, a religious studies graduate, and author of *No Sacred Cows: Investigating Myths, Cults, and the Supernatural*. Mr. McAfee attended University of California, Santa Barbara, and graduated with a dual-degree in English and Religious Studies with an emphasis on Christianity and Mediterranean religions.

Find the author online:

Twitter and Instagram: @DavidGMcAfee

Facebook: @authordavidgmcafee

Website: www.patheos.com/blogs/nosacredcows/

Patreon: www.patreon.com/DavidGMcAfee